Play like a
PRO

What the 50 greatest players can teach you

Edward Craig

hamlyn

For Piper Close and all that have lived in her.

First published in Great Britain in 2007 by
Hamlyn, a division of Octopus Publishing Group Ltd
2–4 Heron Quays, London E14 4JP

Distributed in the United States and Canada by
Sterling Publishing Co., Inc.
387 Park Avenue South, New York, NY 10016-8810

ISBN-13: 978-0-600-61525-5

ISBN-10: 0-600-61525-1

A CIP catalogue record for this book
is available from the British Library

Printed in China

10 9 8 7 6 5 4 3 2 1

Photography shot on location at Burhill Golf Club

Play like a **PRO**

Contents

Introduction

When most golf fans see Tiger Woods smash the ball 365 m (400 yds) down the middle of the fairway, or watch Sergio Garcia land ball after ball close to the hole from around the greens, they wonder how that particular player achieved those shots. The truth is that there is no magic formula, no mysterious touch. The professionals are that good because they possess sound technique, have practised hard and do have a degree of talent beyond others.

This instruction guide gets under the skin of the world's greatest golfers, both past and present. It enables you to get closer to understanding just how the leading professionals play golf by learning about their strengths, listening to their thoughts and tapping into their knowledge. Every element of the game is analysed from the leading players' perspective, so that you can improve your own game and adopt tried-and-tested tips, from how to shape a shot into the green to ways of out-thinking opponents.

This book is a journey through all the legendary golfers, picking out what they did well or how they thought, and then showing you what you can learn from this. I have found a professional who excelled or had a different way of thinking about each particular shot in golf. Phil Mickelson, for example, famously plays wonderful lob shots. Bobby Jones invented modern equipment as well as the US Masters at Augusta, and you will see how his innovations can be best put to use in your own game.

Every golfer would like to hole out putts from 3 m (10 ft) like Tiger Woods, so there are a few tips and hints you can glean from watching his game, which might take you half a step closer to your ambition. Such profiles of the best players will give you a flavour of what they have achieved in general and their greatest feats, as well as what they were like on and off the course. There is analysis of key attributes and insights into these characters, who have made the game of golf so great.

This book is split into chapters, starting with Equipment – you cannot play unless you have got a set of clubs. Other chapters discuss playing golf from the tee, then on the fairway and finally on and around the green. There are also chapters on shot-making and how best to practise your game. Each player profile starts with the history of a player and why he or she is relevant for that particular area of the game. Advice given by these players can be invaluable – they know because they have faced a particular situation and won extensively. The text then provides step-by-step tips, drills and basic advice that you can take from the featured professional, and there are a few pro tips to help and encourage you.

This book is primarily designed to improve your game, yet it will also give you a greater understanding of the history of the sport, how it came to be played as it is and the characters who have made it so colourful and so addictive along the way. An all-round understanding of the game is the quickest way to improve your golf, so get reading.

EDWARD CRAIG

The importance of the right equipment

Bobby Jones left three great legacies in the game of golf. The most famous were designing the Augusta National course, in collaboration with Alister Mackenzie, and founding the annual US Masters there – one of the four majors. What many people do not realize is that Bobby was also the grandfather of modern equipment and mass-market golf. Working with club manufacturers Spalding, he helped design the first set of uniform clubs, which could be machine-produced while retaining a handcrafted feel.

Bobby Jones

Country USA

Born 17 March 1902

Died 18 December 1971

Notable achievements
Open Championship winner 1926, 1927, 1930; US Open winner 1923, 1926, 1929, 1930

Bobby Jones was the sporting colossus in the 1920s. He won a total of 13 major titles (the US and British Amateurs counted as majors at that time) and is the only person to have completed the grand slam of Open Championship, US Open, Amateur Championship and US Amateur in one calendar year (1930). Then, aged 28, he retired from competitive golf to concentrate on a career in law. In 1916, aged 14, Bobby was the youngest player ever to qualify for the US Amateur Championship, and in 1921 he travelled to the UK to play in the Open and the British Amateur Championships. During the Open he displayed a fiery temper while playing the Old Course, at St Andrews, and this endeared him to few. Yet he turned this reputation round with a sensational US Open play-off win against Bobby Cruickshank in 1923, eventually earning the respect of the UK crowd.

Understanding the birth of the modern club

Such was his passion to modernize equipment that Jones rejected more than 200 types before finding the right club design, with steel shafts and, crucially, a number for each club instead of the old Scottish name. Finding the right shaft and understanding how each club works will improve your game enormously.

Pro tip

Always buy the correct modern equipment and take advice from an expert before you do so. Jack Nicklaus said: 'Quality clubs are important', while Lee Trevino countered: 'It is not the arrow, it is the Indian. But an Indian cannot kill anything with a crooked arrow.' You need to have decent technique to make the most of good equipment, but, with poor clubs, it doesn't matter how good your swing is…

Use modern clubs

Jones' mass-produced, steel-shafted models were the forerunners of modern clubs and made the game easier to play. Others have moved designs forward but all from Jones' original vision. Use modern-day designs. Don't become stuck using your grandfather's hand-me-downs.

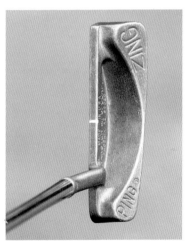

Putter evolution

The next big breakthrough was probably the Ping putter, a design that balanced the head of the putter more naturally, making it easier to putt on quicker greens (a modern thing) without using your wrists. Now there are many designs – this putter opened the door to what was possible.

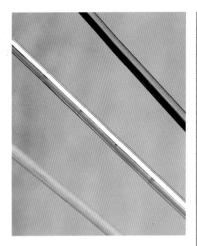

The power of steel

One of the biggest changes to the club was the move from hickory shafts to steel. Hickory was inconsistent and unreliable; the same swing could hit the ball a different distance and with a different ball flight. Steel reacted consistently – the only variable was the person at the end of the club.

Ball development

Increasing the size of the ball, adding dimples and changing materials to improve the feel off the clubface and decrease slices or hooks while adding distance are all innovations that have helped the amateur, so play with a modern ball, selecting one that is best suited to your game (see pages 10–11).

Playing the
right ball

Thomas Bjorn is a typical top-ranking professional. His sponsorship deals not only earn him considerable money but also enable him to play with the best equipment. In 2001, he said that the combination of driver and ball he used gave him an advantage over the rest of the field. Later that year Thomas proved this by beating Tiger Woods in a great contest at the Dubai Desert Classic, having played all 72 holes with Tiger.

Thomas Bjorn

Country Denmark

Born 18 February 1971

Notable achievements
Open Championship runner-up 2000, 2003; US PGA runner-up 2005; Ryder Cup 1997, 2002

Since he graduated from the Challenge Tour in 1996 (eight wins) and competed as the first Dane in two Ryder Cups, Thomas Bjorn has picked up regular victories on the European Tour and has come close to winning major championships. His most agonizing major miss came in the 2003 Open Championship, at Royal St George's, England, where, after leading by two on the 16th tee of the final round, Thomas took three to get out of the bunker, carded a double-bogey and ultimately lost by one stroke to a relatively unknown American, Ben Curtis. It was a bitter blow and it took him 18 months to recover. Since then, Thomas has enjoyed some success on the US PGA Tour and has regained his composure in Europe, where he remains a stalwart senior player.

How to choose a golf ball

Modern players hit the ball so far mainly due to improved ball technology, although the huge-headed drivers have helped consistency in length. Players like Thomas Bjorn spend so much time working out the best ball for their game that they are prepared to admit it gives them an advantage. Different types of balls suit different types of players and conditions.

Best players, top balls

Different types of balls suit different types of players and conditions. Bjorn uses a ball for a big-hitting, pure-striking professional. This may not be ideal for you and can be expensive. Pros use soft, low-spinning balls which means the ball flies far and high while landing softly on the green. Pros have a technique to make the most of the technology.

Balls best suited

Buy a cheaper ball if you are a mid- to high-handicap golfer. This will fly far and will also cope with any mishits you make. A harder ball is much more resilient, and it will travel further from an amateur's swing but should still feel very sweet to strike.

Cheap is cheerful

Select budget-priced hard balls if you are just starting to play golf. Such balls will roll and fly farther than the more costly balls but are more difficult to control when you are a better player. You are liable to lose a few when you are learning and if these are expensive they will not encourage a confident swing.

Play the weather

Consider the conditions on the course and the weather when selecting your ball for a round. If you are playing on a wet or cold day, the ball is not going to fly as far as on a warmer day and will stick into a damp green. You need a hard-shelled ball to bash through the bad weather and beat the cold.

Fairway woods and rescue clubs

At the turn of the 21st century women's golf was dominated by one figure – Karrie Webb. She had won major grand slams, Hall of Fame places and numerous tournaments thanks to her controlled aggression from tee to green. Making the most of modern equipment was essential to Karrie's game. The innovations in fairway woods and rescue clubs, which helped her enormously, are more applicable to amateurs than many other technical advances.

Karrie Webb

Country Australia

Born 21 December 1974

Notable achievements
Weetabix Women's British Open winner 2002; US Women's Open winner 2000, 2001; McDonalds LPGA Championship 2001; Nabisco Championship winner 2000; du Maurier Classic winner 1999

Karrie Webb achieved everything in women's golf younger than anyone else. She was the first Tour rookie on either men's or women's Tours to make $1 million in a season, when she won four events in 1996, during her first year as a professional. Karrie has hardly stopped since then. She has picked up 30 LPGA (Ladies Professional Golf Association) titles and six majors, and became the youngest player to win all four women's majors.

Among other accolades, she has been named Queensland sportswoman of the year on three occasions and she carried the Olympic torch at the Sydney 2000 games. In 2001 she even played with David Duval and Tiger Woods – the then No. 1 and 2 ranked male golfers – alongside Annika Sörenstam in the exhibition match billed as the Battle of Bighorn, an enterprising event only dreamed up because she was so good.

How to select a club to play from the fairway

Hitting a ball the appropriate distance from the fairway is not easy. It requires good technique, a good lie, good shot selection and the right equipment. These days all professional golfers like Karrie Webb have fairway woods and, more than likely, rescue clubs in their bags, and these clubs are especially important for women and amateurs.

Pro tip

Rescue clubs are versatile and can be used not only from 185 m (200 yds) out but also for chipping. The clubhead can bash through wisps of grass to the back of the ball, offering a clean strike whether you are chipping or making a full swing. Overcome those tricky around-the-green lies by pulling out the rescue club.

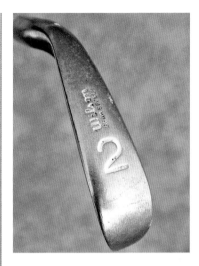

The old-fashioned way

The old-fashioned tool for playing long shots from the fairway was the 1-iron or 2-iron – an impossibly thin piece of metal that offered no forgiveness and was also difficult to get airborne. Nowadays, there is no need to play with anything longer than a 5-iron.

The easy alternative

Fairway woods can offer extra distance over a 1-iron but can also be a substitute for the longer irons. They are easier to hit and get airborne. The extra metal behind the ball and the increased sweet spot make them more forgiving. Karrie and most female professionals will have at least three fairway woods.

The modern way

The rescue club is the new choice for golfers. This is a hybrid fairway wood and long iron, so the head is not as deep or big as the fairway wood, but not as small as an iron. It is a fantastic club to use from tricky lies: the design helps drive to the bottom of the ball without snagging on earth or grass.

The big gamble

The driver is another club that you could use off the fairway if you are feeling very bold. Top professionals will select this club without blinking, but it is tricky to use and requires a solid swing and strike. An amateur is liable to play a cut shot (fading from left to right) if they get the ball airborne at all. But if you use it correctly a driver is a superb club to have.

Selecting
drivers

Liselotte Neumann is one of the great Swedish golfers. She started her professional career on the LET (Ladies European Tour) in the 1980s, then moved on to the US LPGA (Ladies Professional Golf Association) Tour and is still achieving top finishes. Modern equipment certainly helps her, and there is nothing as useful to a golfer as the modern-day driver.

Liselotte Neumann

Country Sweden

Born 20 May 1966

Notable achievements
US Women's Open Championship winner 1988; Solheim Cup 1990, 1992, 1994, 1996, 1998, 2000

Liselotte Neumann has been a flag bearer for European golf for nearly 20 years, and she has also won tournaments around the world – both individual and team events. Having turned professional aged 19 after a successful amateur career, Liselotte won four times on the LET before earning an invite and then qualifying for the LPGA Tour in the USA in 1988. The highlight of her career was winning the US Women's Open Championship in

her rookie year on the US Tour, when aged only 22. She also played in the first six Solheim Cups, helping make that event the competitive three days it is now. Without support from players like Liselotte, the LET may well have disappeared. Liselotte is now based in California, where she has an active on- and off-course life, practising and training hard for tournaments as well as supporting charities and occasionally resting.

How to find the right driver

The women's professional game has much more in common with that of amateurs than the men's, because female professionals hit the ball the same distance and use similar equipment to amateurs. For women like Liselotte Neumann, drives have only got bigger since Callaway launched the first big-headed driver.

Pro tip

Pick up a 12–14 degree loft and ignore the 6–8 degree drivers; then smash the ball past your opponents. This will dispel a golf myth that the lower the loft, the greater the distance you hit the ball. While this may be true with irons, drivers and modern balls are designed to make the ball fly high and long.

The driver revolution

When Liselotte started playing golf, only wooden-headed – or persimmon – drivers existed. These were much smaller in volume than a modern club and, despite being beautifully crafted, were difficult to strike. The advent of metal-headed woods and titanium-headed drivers meant that driving became easier.

Tee it high, watch it fly

Dig out the extra long tees and use the whole of the club's face, because the new drivers are designed to launch the ball up high with little spin, carrying many metres. The deep driver face responds best to a ball struck cleanly with an upward blow, sending the ball skywards.

Make the most of it

Using a modern-day driver is easier but only if you swing it properly. These drivers are big: they have enormous heads, huge faces and large sweet spots, so it is more difficult to mishit than strike sweetly. Yet, if you tee the ball up too low, you'll struggle to make the most of the technological improvement.

Find the best shaft

Modern-day shafts have also helped consistency in ball striking, because the materials and technology used react in the same way for each swing, enabling players to keep their power for longer. Many amateurs will ask for a stiff shaft, in a muscle-bound display of machismo, when their technique and clubhead speed cannot cope. Ask your club professional for the best type of shaft for your swing.

Selecting putters

Ian Woosnam pulled off a remarkable victory in 2001, when he clinched the Cisco World Matchplay title at Wentworth, using a broomhandle putter. He has won the event in three separate decades. A crucial factor in the longevity of such successes has been his choice of putter, which has helped him overcome demons on the greens.

Ian Woosnam

Country Wales

Born 2 March 1958

Notable achievements
US Masters winner 1991; Ryder Cup 1983, 1985, 1987, 1989, 1991, 1993, 1995, 1997, (captain) 2006

Ian Woosnam turned professional in 1976 and was still competing strongly on the European Tour in the early part of the 21st century. He was ranked world No. 1 at the beginning of the 1990s for almost a year, picking up his only major, the US Masters, at that time. Sadly, one of his most famous golfing moments was a calamitous one. Tied for the lead going into the final round of the 2001 Open Championship at Royal Lytham,

Woosie birdied the first hole only to find he had an extra club in his bag, costing him a two-shot penalty. Shaken, he was unable to mount a serious challenge as David Duval claimed the title. That Woosie won the World Matchplay later in the year is testament to his toughness and competitive strength.

How to find the perfect putter

Ian Woosnam flits between a broomhandle and a regular-length putter, depending on the state of his technique. Many older professionals like Ian suffer from the yips which involves a slow loss of nerve when putting. A change in equipment can stall this deterioration. Here are different types of putters and when you might use them.

The three heads

The three types of putterheads are: heel-toe, face-balanced and in-between putter. A heel-toe putter is an old-fashioned bladed club, which can be difficult to use. The face-balanced putter has a bigger head and is more forgiving, while the in-between putter is a mix of both.

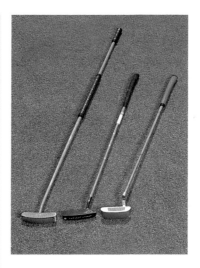

The normal putter

An orthodox-length putter should come up just above your knees, so when you lean over to play the putt, you are comfortable, not too cramped and hunched, and not too stiff and straight. This is the most common length to use.

The broomhandle putter

A broomhandle putter will nearly touch your chin when resting on the ground. The advantage of this is it splits your hands and cuts out the amount of wrist action you use in the stroke. It is invaluable from 3 m (10 ft) and closer, but it can be difficult to judge distances over longer putts.

The belly putter

The belly putter is good for keeping wrists out of the stroke and also for drilling a smooth putting stroke. It is held in the same way as an orthodox-length putter, but its extended shaft anchors in your midriff, keeping the club steady as a pivot point.

Pro tip

Why not carry two putters in your bag – an orthodox-length club for longer putts and a broomhandle for shorter ones? This means you keep the feel for long putts while having that solidity of the broomhandle putter on shorter ones. You are allowed only 14 clubs in your bag if you are not to suffer a two-shot penalty – just ask Ian Woosnam!

Different types of iron clubs

Most touring professionals envy the technical purity of Steve Elkington's golf. This is because of his perfect swing and pure striking. As he hits the ball so cleanly, all he's concerned with is ball flight and spin. To control this best, he uses bladed clubs, which are not forgiving to off-centre strikes.

Steve Elkington

Country Australia

Born 8 December 1962

Notable achievements
US PGA Championship winner 1995

If you had asked a top-level professional through the 1990s whose swing they would most like to have, the majority would have said Steve Elkington's. His technique is a masterpiece, with simple, straight lines blending into a perfect body rotation and pure striking. On top of that, he has enough all-round game to win a major – the US PGA in 1995. He has also won ten titles on the US Tour, he has made numerous President Cup appearances and he has been a fixture in top-level golf for over 15 years. He's won the Vardon Trophy for the lowest scoring average in 1995, and he made 23 from 23 cuts in 1993, making a lot of money in the process. He spends much of his time in Australia as well as his American base in Houston, Texas.

How to select your iron

These are of two basic types: bladed and cavity-backed. To make the most of bladed irons, you have to be a pure ball striker like Steve Elkington. Most amateur players tend to use the less penetrative cavity-backed irons, which are more forgiving for off-centre strikes.

The old club

In the 1960s, there was only one type of iron – the blade. This beautifully crafted club with razor-like edges is difficult to strike. The sweet spot is small, and the margin for error smaller. If you miss the middle of the club by a fraction, you will feel it in your hands and see it as the ball travels half the distance.

When old meets new

A modern bladed iron with its straight back still needs a pure strike. Such a club feels great when you make good contact, and you have control of the ball flight. When used properly, bladed irons make it easier to punch the ball low, draw or fade. If you get the strike wrong, the results can be poor and painful.

Forgive and forget

Cavity-backed irons have a hollowed section at the back of the head, lowering the centre of gravity and increasing the size of the sweet spot. This makes it easier to get the ball airborne, and you will not suffer too badly for off-centre strikes. You cannot manipulate the ball flight as easily as with a blade, though.

Mix and match

Modern hybrid sets of clubs are now available. In these, the shorter irons are more blade-like, and so easier to control, while the longer irons are more cavity-backed in design, so it is simpler to get the ball airborne and flying straight. This gives you the best of both worlds, forgiveness and penetration, but they do tend to be more expensive.

Pro tip

Only top players may be able to tell the difference between cast-iron clubs and forged ones, especially now that modern casting techniques have been vastly improved. Cast-iron clubs are made by pouring molten metal into a mould, while forged clubs are made from a soft steel, stamped into a basic shape and finished by hand.

An extra wedge

Phil Mickelson has been one of the world's top four golfers since the end of the 1990s. Aside from his being left-handed, the distinctive element to his game is his versatility around the greens, because of the range of chip-and-pitch shots he can play with such accuracy. A lot of this versatility can be put down to the extra wedge Phil adds to his bag.

Phil Mickelson

Country USA

Born 16 June 1970

Notable achievements
US Masters winner 2004, 2006;
US PGA winner 2005

Phil Mickelson won a professional event as an amateur (the 1991 Northern Telecom Open) and then throughout the rest of the 1990s and early part of the 21st century he consistently picked up tournaments on the US PGA Tour, but seemed doomed never to make that major breakthrough. This incredibly talented golfer, raised in Arizona, was famous for his all-out aggression, which was great to watch but landed him in too much trouble. A calmer and more assured Mickelson appeared at the 2004 US Masters. By playing conservatively, driving accurately and producing his reliable impressive short game, Phil claimed his first major. In 2005 he had added a second major, claiming the US PGA title, and a third one in 2006, at the US Masters again. Phil is one of the modern American superstars – frustrating, flawed and genius in equal measure.

How to select a wedge

When amateurs think of adding extra clubs to their bags, they will usually select another wood or long iron. Professionals know which part of the game makes them most money and so they select another wedge. Phil Mickelson has four wedges to cover every eventuality, every lie and every obstacle.

The pitching wedge

Use a pitching wedge when you are 110 m (120 yds) or closer from the green, and pitch when there is green between the ball and flag. Most normal wedges have a 48-degree loft, but Phil's pitching wedge has a 45-degree one, as he likes uniformity in his wedge lofts to stop him being between clubs.

The gap wedge

Use a gap wedge for full shots from 90 m (100 yds). This will reduce the need to hit a half pitching wedge or hard sand-wedge into the green. You can maintain your tempo and make a good full swing with the right club, rather than manipulating a shot. Typically, a gap wedge has a 52-degree loft (Phil's is 50).

The sand-wedge

Use a sand-wedge as a full club from 73–90 m (80–100 yds) or when you need to lob the ball high at the flag and not have too much run. It is the major club for getting out of bunkers and has a specially rounded bottom, and helps your escape. Typically a sand-wedge has a 56-degree loft, although Phil's is 55.

The lob-wedge

Use a lob-wedge to loft the ball high without moving it far forward and land it softly on the green. It also helps you make a full swing from 55–73 m (60–80 yds), where a half sand-wedge is difficult to control. This newest and most dangerous of wedges requires practice to use with confidence but can have spectacular results. Phil uses the traditional 60-degree loft.

Pro tip

Buy specialist wedges; don't just use the ones that came with your set. Wedges are like putters and drivers: you have to find one that suits you. They come in many shapes and colours – black, silver, rusted – and each has different properties. Find which feels best for you. That extra wedge in your bag will lower your scores.

The first
modern grip

Harry Vardon was the first golfing celebrity. At the beginning of the 20th century, he dominated the Open Championship, winning it six times, and he also toured the United States, where he won the US Open in 1900. All modern greats are still judged by the standards he set.

Harry Vardon

Country England

Born 9 May 1870

Died 20 March 1937

Notable achievements
Open Championship winner 1896, 1898, 1899, 1903, 1911, 1914; US Open winner 1900

Harry Vardon is a colossus in the history of golf not only for his achievements in major tournaments – no one has beaten his six Open triumphs – but also for his technical legacy. Harry pioneered the overlapping (or Vardon) grip, which is now used by 70 per cent of golfers in the world. He grew up in Jersey, playing the Victorian version of pitch-and-putt – a small course, with only short holes – and working as a gardener, before coming to England to try 'proper' golf. He won his first event, came second in his next and turned pro. Harry beat the dominant golfer of the time, J.H. Taylor, to win his first Open in 1896. In 1903 he suffered tuberculosis, which gave him a jittery putting stroke – although he did win two more Opens. After his death, the US PGA Tour introduced the Vardon Trophy, an annual award for the player with the lowest scoring average.

How to make the Vardon grip

Harry Vardon did not invent the Vardon (or overlapping) grip, but popularized it. He used his hands as one solid unit, with neither the right nor the left having more influence over the clubface. Most problems in the swing originate from a faulty grip, so get this right and you will make life easier. A key to any good grip is the tension, or lack of it, in your hold.

1 Stand upright and let your hands hang naturally by your sides. Then ask a friend to place the club in your left hand, without changing the position. Let the club rest at the base of your fingers, and not in the palm of your hand, with the V of your hand pointing to your right collarbone.

2 Allow the thumb on the left hand to slide down the shaft of the club by about 1.5 cm (½ in). Then place your right hand on the club, positioning the little finger of your right hand over the gap between your index and next finger on your left. Again, make sure the grip runs along the base of your fingers, and not in your palms.

3 Make sure that the V between your thumb and index finger on both hands points to your right collarbone. If it does not, you will have either a strong or a weak grip. which will lead to an open or closed clubface at impact.

4 Ensure you hold the club gently: that is, firmly enough to keep control but lightly enough for a friend to pull it from your hands with a sharp tug.

Pro tip

An often-overlooked element when building a decent grip is the thickness of the grip on the shaft. Most amateurs will find a thick grip more comfortable because it is soft and can be held more tightly, but this will tighten the rest of your swing. Ask your local professional if the thickness of your grip is right for the size of your hands.

Two further grips

Ben Hogan's most famous triumph was the only Open Championship that he ever played in, at Carnoustie in 1953. He tamed the wild links with such aggression and strength that the par-five sixth hole became known as Hogan's Alley after Ben consistently took the high-risk, high-reward route – claiming a birdie each round.

Ben Hogan

Country USA

Born 13 August 1912

Died 25 July 1997

Notable achievements
Open Championship winner 1953; US Masters winner 1951, 1953; US Open winner 1948, 1950, 1951, 1953; US PGA winner 1946, 1948; Ryder Cup 1947, 1951

Ben Hogan was not only one of the most successful golfers of all time but he also wrote one of the most influential books on the golf swing, *Five lessons: the modern fundamentals of golf*, which can be found in many top pros' lockers and is a bedrock for much teaching philosophy and thinking. He was a famed striker of the ball and was dedicated to the practice range. Ben's career was also remarkable for its success over adversity. In 1949 he suffered a near-fatal car crash and doctors thought he might never walk again. Yet 11 months later Ben was playing golf again at the top level, only losing in a play-off to Sam Snead at the Los Angeles Open. In 1953 he won five out of the six events he entered, including the first three majors of the year.

How to make the interlocking grip

'Golf begins with a good grip,' wrote Ben Hogan in his famous instruction manual. 'The grip is the heartbeat of the golf swing.' That said, he does concede there are different and equally successful methods of holding the club. The most popular alternative to the Vardon grip is the interlocking grip, which Ben Hogan also advocated.

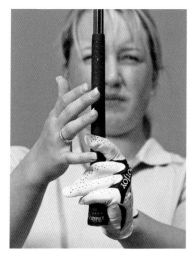

1 Take hold of the club with your left hand as you would for the Vardon grip (see pages 22–23), with the thumb pointing down the shaft.

2 Interlock the little finger of the right hand with the index finger of the left, hooking them together. Keep the grip running through the base of your fingers, not your palms, and shuffle until comfortable, with the Vs pointing to your right collarbone, as for the Vardon grip.

3 Practise your grip daily by making, then remaking it. No need for a club; just practise working your hands together. Ben wrote: 'In golf, there are certain things you must do quite precisely, where being approximately right is not right enough. The grip is one of those areas where being half-right accomplishes nothing.'

Baseball or ten-finger grip

Take hold of the club in your left hand as you would for building any other grip. Then slide your right hand on as before, but instead of linking your hands with fingers touching, leave them unconnected. If anything, let your left thumb sit under the palm of the right hand – although this is not essential.

Pro tip

The aim of your grip is to hold the club in such a way that your hands act as a unit, keeping the clubface square to the target throughout the swing and at impact. Your grip is your only connection with the club so it is the most important element. More swing problems originate from a dodgy grip than from any other element of the technique.

Perfect
posture

Justin Rose burst into international golf when, as a 17-year-old amateur, he came fourth in the Open Championship in 1998. He immediately turned professional and struggled. His battle finished in an emotional event in Johannesburg four years later, when he won his first professional tournament, the Dunhill Championship. He is one of a number of emerging British golfers making headway on both sides of the Atlantic and appears to have the talent and technique to take it that step further – but does he have the temperament?

Justin Rose

Country England

Born 30 July 1980

Notable achievements
Open Championship fourth 1998

Justin Rose's story is one of triumph, followed by disaster and then rebuilding. His 1998 Open Championship probably hindered rather than helped – he rushed into tournament golf and missed 21 consecutive cuts. But he slowly established himself on satellite tours with the help of David Leadbetter and his father Ken, who died of leukemia in 2002. Justin now plays predominantly on the US PGA Tour, where he is a popular figure. His attachment to the US PGA Tour, however, restricts his chances of qualifying for the European team in the Ryder Cup. Yet it is only a matter of time before he forces his way onto the team, via major finishes or a captain's pick.

How to develop good posture

Justin's hard learning curve in professional golf has taught him how to cope under pressure. But his swing relies on outstanding basics that he returns to whenever he is feeling the heat, or not swinging quite right. He has superb athletic posture at address, which is essential for an explosive powerful swing. Develop good posture with this step-by-step guide.

1 Stand up straight with the ball in the correct position, just forward of centre in your stance. Using a good grip, hold a mid-iron at a 45-degree angle to your arms in front of you. Place your feet a shoulder's width apart, with your toes slightly turned out.

2 Keep your back and knees straight and bend from the hips, letting the club drop to the ground behind the ball. Don't change the angle between your arms and the club but only hinge at your waist. Let your arms hang naturally underneath your shoulders.

3 From this position flex your knees and let your bottom stick out. Imagine you are balancing a full wine glass on the base of your spine. Keep your back straight and retain softness in your knees; you want to be in a stable and firm position. The club rests behind the ball and your hands are below your shoulders, not reaching forward.

4 Try to find a comfortable and athletic position, which is the aim of good posture. You want to be stable enough to make an athletic turn at the ball without losing the shape of the swing because you have lifted your spine or straightened and tensed your knees too much. You need to stay loose and flexible but stable.

Pro tip

Using a mirror to check your posture is a great way to keep your technique sharp. Check that your back is straight and there is enough flex in your knees. A good posture will maintain your decent swing as you play more golf. Solid fundamentals are simple in thought and execution, so will not fail you under pressure.

Backing the basics

Tiger Woods is the best golfer in the world and could well be the best player ever to have swung a club. His dominance at the end of the 1990s and start of the 21st century was so great that at one time he held all four major titles. As with all great players, he does the simple things brilliantly.

Tiger Woods

Country USA

Born 30 December 1975

Notable achievements
Open Championship winner 2000, 2005, 2006; US Masters winner 1997, 2001, 2002, 2005; US Open winner 2000, 2002; US PGA winner 1999, 2000, 2006; Ryder Cup 1997, 1999, 2002, 2004

From an early age Tiger Woods was touted for success. At the age of three, he shot 48 over nine holes; then he broke scoring records and won events regularly as an amateur. This culminated in three US Amateur titles before he turned professional and won the Las Vegas International in his first season in 1996. His first major victory came at the US Masters the following year, where he blew away the field to win by a record 12 shots. Tiger has taken golf to a new level, placing added emphasis on fitness and nutrition, as well as constantly working hard at his own game. He has undergone two swing revamps in his professional life, emerging a stronger and better player each time.

How to adopt a good ball position and stance

Tiger Woods' sound fundamentals are the basis for his extraordinary consistency mixed with power, and he accurately maintains his stance and ball position whatever the situation. His driver is one of his greatest weapons so his technique is spot on with this club. Here is a drill to help you find a good ball position.

1 Take a driver and tee up a ball. Stand with your feet close together, holding the club out so it rests behind the ball. You want to keep the ball opposite your left heel when using a driver; don't let it slip too far back. Grip the club as normal and maintain good posture throughout, trying to keep the clubface square to the target line.

2 Move your right foot back, leaving your left foot where it started. Place your feet a shoulder's width apart, by moving your right foot only, and turn your toes out slightly. If anything, build a base that is marginally wider than your shoulders, but remember you are looking to stay comfortable and remain balanced.

3 Ensure the ball is opposite your left heel. This is the perfect position for a driver. You are looking to catch the ball on the up-section of your swing, launching it high down the fairway. If the ball creeps back, you may catch it on the down section, which will lead to an inconsistent strike and ball flight.

4 If you are playing a mid-iron, position the ball forward of centre, and with a short iron the ball should be played central in the stance. The shorter the club, the further back the ball position and the steeper the angle of attack, so you catch the ball with a more downward blow.

Pro tip

The height at which players tee the ball dictates the ball flight. With modern, big-headed drivers, it is imperative to tee the ball high. Modern clubs are designed to launch the ball with a high rainbow-shaped flight, not with the low-rising flight of old clubs. So tee it high and use that big-headed driver to hit it high and far.

Good
alignment

Padraig Harrington is one of Europe's biggest stars, and he always plays with a smile on his face. Along with his nine European Tour victories, he has also won twice on the US PGA Tour – the Honda Classic and the Barclays Classic, both in 2005 – where he is an ever-popular figure, too.

Padraig Harrington

Country Ireland

Born 31 August 1971

Notable achievements
Ryder Cup 1999, 2002, 2004

Padraig Harrington is one of the hardest-working professional golfers in the world, and is probably outshone only by Vijay Singh for the hours he has spent on the range. Since 1999, all the practice has paid off. He sneaked into the Ryder Cup team that year in tenth place and has not looked back, the following year winning his first tournament since 1996. Padraig has not quite had the volume of wins his talent merits, but has achieved numerous runner-up spots, including four in 1999, as well as top-five finishes in four majors. He enjoyed a successful amateur career, playing in the Walker Cup side three times, including in the victorious 1995 side. Padraig completed an accountancy degree before turning professional, which gave him a taste of real life outside the golfing circus, an attribute that is ever present.

How to hit straight

Padraig Harrington will spend hours on the range practising the basics, drilling the fundamental techniques that make his swing so consistent. Correct alignment – the direction in which your body and club aim – is an essential element to hitting good, accurate, straight shots.

1 To hit the ball straight, the clubface must be square to the target at impact. To give yourself the best chance of returning the club to this position, you need to start with the clubface square at address. Look down your target line and pick a point – a mark on the ground – a few metres in front of the clubface on that line.

2 Place your club on the ground so the face aims directly at this one spot. Now build the rest of your stance around this good accurate position, making sure that your shoulders, knees, hips and toes are all perfectly parallel to this target line.

3 To help envisage good alignment, picture a set of train tracks running from the target to your ball. Your ball is on one line of the tracks, the same one as your target line. Your feet and shoulders are on the other. Your shoulders should be parallel to the target line, just like these imaginary tracks; they should not point directly at it.

4 Even if you are working on another element of your technique, you should still practise good alignment. If you were to watch Padraig on the range, you would see him working with the train track imagery. He will always have a couple of clubs laid out on the ground, one running along his toe line, the other just inside, but parallel to, the target line. These act as a guide for every shot he plays.

Pro tip

Certain coaches say that around half of the wild shots amateurs play are a result of poor alignment, not of poor technique. For example, if the ball goes 45 m (50 yds) wide after you have made a good swing with good preparation, this is because you were inadvertently aiming for that spot. Always practise alignment to iron out this problem.

The first movement

Retief Goosen would be known as the most elegant South African golfer were it not for his golfing compatriot Ernie Els. His smooth technique and tempo are one of the most picturesque sights in professional golf, and his easy-going, off-course demeanour matches his relaxed and natural swing. He is one of the modern greats who can actually challenge Tiger Woods' dominance.

Retief Goosen

Country South Africa

Born 3 February 1969

Notable achievements
US Open winner 2001, 2004

Retief Goosen emerged at the beginning of the 2000s as a contender for the world's top spots. Until then he had battled hard on the European Tour, winning a handful of events – usually in France – before making his major breakthrough at the 2001 US Open. Then, in 2004, he proved this was no fluke, by seeing off a late charge from that year's US Masters champion, Phil Mickelson, to pick up his second title. Retief has a reputation for making mistakes under pressure: for example, he blew a three-shot lead in the final round of the 2005 US Open. He was the first non-European to win the Order of Merit since Greg Norman in 1982, and then successfully defended his crown the following year. Retief was struck by lightning as an amateur and suffered health problems as a consequence, which delayed his development into one of the world's best golfers till later in life.

How to follow Goosen's first movement

Retief Goosen says that he likes to keep the swing as simple as possible: 'I do not like to think of too many things when I am playing golf.' He has fantastic fundamentals, posture, grip, stance, which help him keep the swing consistent, and his swing is all about an easy rhythm and tempo. The first movement is essential when kick-starting this easy action.

1 Have one simple swing thought on each shot, to keep your technique tight. The key to a good takeaway is to take the club back slow and low. If this is your one swing thought, it will help you build consistent rhythm as well as create a good wide arc in your backswing.

2 Take the club back gently by turning your shoulders and back to the target. Don't snatch the club away quickly, or lift it with your arms too early in the swing.

3 Keep your address position and setup square and parallel to the target, and maintain this through the swing. Keep the clubface pointing at the target for the first metre of the swing before turning your shoulders. Don't pull the club inside the target line or push your hands outside it.

Simple takeaway drill

Place a tee peg in the ground 60 cm (2 ft) behind the ball and directly on the target line. As you take the club away from the ball, try to brush the top of this tee. Practise until this correct movement becomes second nature and you are no longer prone to taking the club away on the inside or out.

Pro tip

The slow, low, takeaway movement back must also be smooth. Keep your width in the swing and generate the Goosen-esque easy rhythm with this first movement of the club. Don't jerk the club back aggressively with your wrists.

The X factor

In the final round of the 1996 US Masters, Nick Faldo overturned his six-shot deficit to win by five. He slowly dismantled the game and mind of the leader, Greg Norman, by piling on the pressure through consistent nerveless golf, exemplified by his second shot into the par-five 13th, a notorious high-risk, high-reward hole. He struck a 2-iron into the heart of the green, guaranteeing a birdie and breaking Greg's final resistance.

Nick Faldo

Country England

Born 18 July 1957

Notable achievements
Open Championship winner 1987, 1990, 1992; US Masters winner 1989, 1990, 1996; Ryder Cup 1977, 1979, 1981, 1983, 1985, 1987, 1989, 1991, 1993, 1995, 1997

Nick Faldo is still one of the most recognizable names and faces in world golf today. He has won six major titles, numerous US and European Tour events, and has gained more Ryder Cup points than any other player. Nick has also made considerable money in off-course golf businesses such as coaching academies and course design. He famously rebuilt his golf swing from scratch under the tutelage of David Leadbetter, when he realized his current technique was too loose under the extreme pressure of the closing holes of a major. Although heavily criticized at the time for making such radical changes, Nick went on to win six titles when he returned to professional golf. The famous 2-iron shot at the 1996 US Masters typified the new solidity and control he discovered with his new technique.

How to play consistent golf

Nick Faldo developed an incredibly reliable technique, and the X factor was a central element. It is a vital technique for consistency. Nick's technical control is masterful as demonstrated by that 2-iron. On the tee any technical flaws are ruthlessly exposed, so you should work on this fundamental element of your game. You will then hit many more fairways.

1 At the top of your backswing, rotate your shoulders through 90 degrees from where they started. This is a simple yet flexible position – the tip of the left shoulder points at the ball and, crucially, the head moves so you look at the ball out of your left eye. Don't try to keep your head still as this restricts your movement.

2 Rotate the lower body around 45 degrees; don't turn it as far as the shoulders. This is the X-factor technique that Nick worked on with David Leadbetter. By rotating the shoulders 90 degrees and the lower body 45 degrees, you use your big reliable muscles to swing the club, and the movement is consistent.

3 If you draw a line through your hips and through your shoulders, then take a bird's-eye view, you will see an X – this is the X factor, the difference between your upper and lower body rotation. The greater the difference, the greater the resistance and the more power you will generate.

4 Once you have found this coiled reliable position, all you have to do is uncoil and let your shoulders, back and thighs guide the club into the back of the ball. Not that much can go wrong with these big muscles, so your ball striking becomes consistent and extremely powerful, whatever the match situation.

Pro tip

Nick rotated his shoulders 90 degrees and his hips 45 – this is a top athletic golfer – so don't be too concerned if you cannot be as flexible. Make sure there is some difference between your lower and upper body positions, so you are not turning your entire body behind the ball as one, which is the old-fashioned and less reliable method.

The transition

One of the most distinctive and exciting swings in the professional game is Sergio Garcia's. He is a young, athletic golfer with a unique loop at the top of his backswing, which creates enormous explosive power. Sergio has won six times on the US PGA Tour and has consistently been Europe's top-ranked player since 2001.

Sergio Garcia

Country Spain

Born 9 January 1980

Notable achievements
US PGA 1999 runner-up; Ryder Cup 1999, 2002, 2004

Sergio Garcia had an astonishing amateur career, which included winning a professional tournament, the Catalonian Open, as a 17-year-old. He turned professional in 1999, aged 19, and later that year stunned the crowds at the PGA Championship, when he challenged the leader, Tiger Woods. Since then, controversy (to do with his ill temper) and technical difficulties in his swing have restricted Sergio in major championships. He has undergone technical adjustments, which is always difficult with such an instinctive and natural technique. He wins regularly on the US PGA Tour, where he is now based, and is a crowd pleaser with a big-hitting, gung-ho attitude, mixed with delicacy of touch around the greens, including brilliant and dreadful putting in equal measure.

How to work on the transition

There are elements of Sergio Garcia's technique that you can learn from, even if his swing is no technical masterpiece. It is the source of much power. At the top of his backswing, his weight has turned to his right side and his back faces the target. From here, backswing turns to downswing as he shifts his weight from the right to the left side.

1 Start your downswing with your hips rotating left and triggering your upper body to uncoil.

2 Move your left shoulder away from your chin. The weight will then transfer to the left side, and a chain reaction should bring the club powerfully down behind the ball.

3 Start the downswing with the lower body, then everything else will follow. Garcia has a loop in his backswing, which means his body is ahead of his arms in the transition. This is an exaggeration of letting the lower body start the downswing through shifting your weight to your left.

4 Adopt Sergio's transition technique into your swing, so you avoid leading the downswing with your right shoulder, which is a common cause of slicing.

Pro tip

A good practice drill, which you can incorporate into your pre-shot routine, is to swing to the top of your backswing, pause for a fraction of a second, then make your transition and stop. Drill the feeling of dropping the club with nothing more than force of gravity, and this pause will force your lower body to start the downswing.

The importance of rhythm

Sam Snead emerged in 1937 as a talented country boy, driving the ball further than any of his contemporaries and earning the nickname 'Slammin' Sam'. He was blessed with the most beautiful natural rhythm and a swing that kept him in professional golf longer than any other player.

Sam Snead

Country USA

Born 27 May 1912

Died 23 May 2002

Notable achievements
US Masters 1949, 1952, 1954;
Open Championship winner 1946;
US PGA winner 1942, 1949, 1951;
Ryder Cup 1937, 1947, 1949,
1951, 1953, 1955, 1959

Sam Snead achieved more than 130 professional victories worldwide, including 82 US PGA Tour wins. In 1950 he won 11 times, the last time a golfer has posted double-digit victories in a season. But it is the longevity of his career that is even more astonishing. Sam was the first golfer to beat his age, when aged 67 he shot 67 and 66 at the Quad Cities Open 1979, and he was actively involved in setting up the Seniors Tour

in 1979. He would never practise as hard as his rivals, and instead relied on his natural rhythm for consistency and power. Sam once observed: 'If a lot of people gripped a knife and fork the way they do a golf club, they'd starve to death.' He remained an honorary starter for the US Masters until the year of his death, in 2002.

How to make a rhythmic swing

Sam Snead's rhythm was the envy of professionals around the world. With seemingly effortless power, he hit the ball miles as all his muscles worked in perfect synchronization. He also displayed the grace of a dancer. According to Jack Nicklaus: 'Watching Sam Snead practise hitting balls is like watching a fish practise to swim.'

1 Smooth your rhythm by counting in your swing. Count 'one' on the backswing, and 'two' on the throughswing. Nick Faldo actually says 'Sam' on his backswing and then 'Snead' on the way down.

2 Ensure your swing is a long, fluid motion needing timing and tempo. Much of golf is working on positions, staying in plane, having the right angle of attack. Don't work on good positions on the backswing at the expense of your natural rhythm. You may have perfect positions but they have to knit together in one motion.

3 Don't be afraid to play a natural, free-flowing game in practice and on the course. Snead did not work hard at his game; he only did what he needed to keep everything in natural and simple order. He once said: 'Thinking instead of acting is the No. 1 golf disease.' He relied on a natural swing and instinct.

4 Try a practice session with music to improve your tempo, using musical beats to work on your game and help you develop a natural timing. 'I always enjoy dancing. It helped me learn and value rhythm and grace,' Snead explained. He admitted that the 1-2-3 waltz beat kept his timing in synchronization.

Pro tip
Don't fight what comes naturally to you, because every golfer has a different tempo and rhythm. These often depend on the type of personality. Ernie Els is a laid-back person and has a relaxed swing, while Nick Price is a hectic character and has an up-tempo technique as a result.

The moment of impact

David Duval was the first golfer seriously to challenge Tiger Woods' global dominance at the end of the 1990s. For a brief period, he even ousted Woods from the world No. 1 slot. With a typical, relaxed, natural and confident display, David won the 2001 Open Championship at Royal Lytham. He was swinging so well that he was not going to make any mistakes on the back nine on the final day, and despite starting the day in a four-way tie he carved out a three-shot win.

David Duval

Country USA

Born 9 November 1971

Notable achievements
Open Championship winner 2001; Ryder Cup 1999, 2002

David Duval is an aggressive, focused golfer who can shoot extremely low numbers when his game is on. He is one of three players to score 59 in a US PGA Tour event, when he eagled the last at the Bob Hope Chrysler Classic in 1999. Sadly, though, since his major triumph in 2001, David's form has disappeared. A combination of personal problems and injuries has led to numerous missed cuts, long periods out of the game and the intermittent low score. In 2005 he made one cut in 20 starts. There have been fleeting signs of a resurgence at regular intervals, but nothing sustained. David is famous for his cool, unflappable manner and dark sunglasses, and a return to the pin-killing form of 2001 would be very welcome.

How to achieve a good impact position

When David Duval was at his best, his free-flowing swing was a result of a great impact position. Impact is the most important moment – and David's head position is distinct and a lesson to all amateur golfers, for one simple reason. A classic mistake in the golf swing – the biggest myth and most common error – is to try to keep your head down.

1 Turn your head at impact (and on the backswing) by letting your eyes follow the clubhead, then the ball, to free your swing up. This is what David does. Don't get stuck looking at the ground for seconds after impact (as pictured).

2 David is so keen to let his swing flow and not be restricted by a still head that he does not look at the ball at impact. His head has moved and his eyes are looking a few metres in front of the ball as he makes contact.

3 Try hitting a pillow or old sofa cushion to drill a good impact position. This offers resistance, stopping the clubhead suddenly (but softly) as you strike. It forces you into a good pillow-impact position. Let your head go as you strike, whacking a pillow, while developing good technique.

Drill for natural rhythm and flow to the swing

Place a line of six balls on tees running directly away from you. Then walk down the line hitting each ball in turn, without resetting your address. Just enjoy the flow and liberation of rhythmically and naturally hitting balls as you walk down the line. This drill will improve your impact position.

Pro tip

It does not matter what your swing looks like, or how many mistakes you are making at address or in your backswing, as long as the club meets the ball square at impact. You are more likely to achieve this if every other part of your swing is in good shape.

The need for clubhead speed

Nick Price

Country Zimbabwe

Born 28 January 1957

Notable achievements
Open Championship winner 1994;
US PGA winner 1992, 1994

Nick Price is a golfer of remarkable longevity: he has competed at the top level of professional golf for nearly 30 years. His three major triumphs came in a four-year golden patch, when he topped the US money list in 1993 and 1994. He is one of only three players to win two majors in a year in the 1990s, alongside Nick Faldo and Mark O'Meara, and he won more tournaments than any other player in that decade. More recently, Nick has set up a golf course design company. He still plays and makes good money on the US PGA Tour, where he rarely misses cuts and rarely makes mistakes. He is as affable off the course as he is dynamic on it, and is a favourite with the press, who in 2002 awarded him a prize for quotability, cooperation and accommodation.

How to improve clubhead speed

All amateur golfers can boost their clubhead speed, to increase the distance they hit the ball and the efficiency of their swing. Clubhead speed is about one thing: how fast you swing the club. The faster you swing, the further the ball flies and the more power you have in your game.

The heavy club

Swing two clubs at once. Although the added weight will make it tough to take the clubs back and swing them through naturally, force yourself to do it as many times as possible. Then swing with one club; it will feel light and easy to swing quickly. Many coaches have an extra heavy club in their training bag to help with this.

The light club

An alternative to this drill is to use the club the wrong way round. Grab hold of the clubhead and swing the grip, to give you the effect of swinging an extra light club. Swing quickly so you make a positive 'whoosh' noise as the grip cuts through the air. To keep improving your speed, make this noise louder and louder.

Using his famously quick tempo, Nick Price won the 1994 Open Championship and US PGA in a year that took him to the world No. 1 spot. He snaps through his swing quickly, with an efficient, tightly controlled action that has few moving parts, which means that not much can go wrong under pressure.

Pro tip

Swing speed comes not just from added strength but also from increased flexibility. Being strong and flexible are essential attributes for golf. Although they do not look the most athletic players, John Daly and Colin Montgomerie are extremely flexible and can touch their toes and tie themselves in knots. This is their natural gift.

1 Start the swing with the club held 60 cm (2 ft) in front of the ball. Address the ball as before but place the clubhead off the ground and in front of the ball.

2 Make a natural swing back from this position to the top of your backswing. By moving your club ahead of the ball, you will give your backswing more momentum as you turn – you will naturally generate more pace thanks to the added distance the club has to travel. Your downswing will replicate this speed and you will hit the ball further.

The follow-through

Colin Montgomerie has won eight European Tour Order of Merits including seven in succession from 1993 to 1999. His relaxed rhythmical swing, with its distinct finish position, is part of his natural and unteachable technique, although many of the fundamentals behind it are applicable to everyone.

Colin Montgomerie

Country Scotland

Born 23 June 1963

Notable achievements
Open Championship runner-up 2005; US Open runner-up 1994, 1997; US PGA runner-up 1995; Ryder Cup 1991, 1993, 1995, 1997, 1999, 2002, 2004

Colin Montgomerie is one of the most popular golfers in Europe, commanding huge respect for his achievements on the golf course, despite the lack of major titles, and for his friendly and approachable manner off it. His greatest exploits have been in the Ryder Cup, where he has never been defeated in a singles match and where he holed the winning putt in the 2004 event. He suffered a loss of form when his marriage publicly failed in the 2003 season. Then, languishing in the world rankings at the start of 2005, he aimed high and won the Order of Merit for an astonishing eighth time, including coming second to Tiger Woods in the Open Championship at St Andrews. Monty is involved in many off-course projects, including course design and a coaching academy at Turnberry, which is near Royal Troon, where his father was Secretary and Monty first learned golf.

How to follow Monty's follow-through

Colin Montgomerie's swing is unique and unrepeatable for mere mortals. It has great rhythm and is good to watch but technically it is peculiar. Yet, for Monty, it is repeatable and controllable – and what more do you need? That distinct finish position, though, holds a few secrets.

1 Never hit at the ball but swing through it. If you hit at the ball you will use too much hand and arm in the swing. Monty tries to have only 75 per cent of his weight on his left side at impact, then just before his finish position the rest of the weight follows. He says he does not 'finish' hitting the ball until he has ended his follow-through.

2 Have a mirror image of your backswing in your throughswing. When Monty turns his back to the target on the backswing, he wants to turn his chest to the target in the throughswing. Left arm is across the chest on the backswing, right arm across the chest on the way through.

3 Rehearse a good finish, to help you find that balanced and strong position more naturally. It is difficult to fake a good finish. If you have made a poor swing, you will be off balance, with your hands below your head or you will be stumbling over the shot (as pictured).

Drill for a good strong finish

Monty has four swing thoughts that he returns to if he is off kilter: swing back slow and low; complete the backswing; start down with a move of the hips; and swing to a full-balanced finish. This simple good advice is applicable to anyone. Think to swing to a strong finish and you will make a good strike.

Pro tip

It is important to release your hands in the throughswing, which means turning your forearms and wrists over through impact and beyond. You will be surprised how much extra power this gives you. This is the only moment of the swing when your arms should be fully extended, so let that release happen and enjoy the flow.

Tee tactics

Annika Sörenstam

Country Sweden

Born 9 October 1970

Notable achievements
Kraft Nabisco Championship winner 2001, 2002, 2005; LPGA Championship winner 2003, 2004, 2005; US Women's Open Championship winner 1995, 1996; Weetabix British Open winner 2003; Solheim Cup 1994, 1996, 1998, 2000, 2002, 2003, 2005

Following a highly successful amateur career, Annika Sörenstam turned professional in 1992 and won her first two majors, the US Women's Open Championship, in 1995 and 1996. But this was not enough. Annika wanted to be beyond unbeatable. Around the end of the 1990s she hit the gym and practice range harder than ever before, resulting in a robotic and powerful golfer. She shot the first competitive 59 in women's golf in the Standard Register Ping event in 2001.

Then Annika picked up a further seven majors, completing a grand slam over the next five years – and she does not look like stopping. She was the first female golfer invited to play on the men's US PGA Tour when she competed in the Colonial Tournament in 2003. Annika missed the cut but paved the way for women to take on the men in tournament golf.

How to improve your tee tactics

Annika Sörenstam makes few mistakes and this is because she is such a thoughtful golfer, playing intelligently from the tee. She simply plays the percentage shots, and does not take big risks or fall for any of the temptations or tricks of the course. Every shot is played to put her in the best position for the next.

1 Pick a specific point in the distance as your target, when playing a tee shot. Look at a branch of a tree or a particular marking on a bunker; don't choose a whole tree or whole bunker for a target line. If you miss a specific point by 20 per cent, you will be in good shape. Miss a general target by 20 per cent and you are in trouble.

2 Tee up on the same side as the trouble, so you hit away from it, if you are playing a hole with, say, water down the right side or with trees tight down the left. Don't stand on the opposite side of the tee box, looking at the hazard in a terrified way, as you will then be hitting at it. Use the complete width of the tee to your advantage.

Annika Sörenstam has done to women's golf what Tiger Woods has done to men's: dominated it. Her all-round game is so solid and so much better than that of any of her contemporaries that it is difficult to pick out one particular excellence. She just never misses.

Pro tip

Developing a game plan for each hole is essential to low scoring. Even more important is sticking to it. Don't be tempted to pull out a driver on a hole you wanted to play with an iron, because you feel the match situation requires a big shot.

3 Mentally play the hole backwards. Work out where you would like to make your birdie putt from on the green, then work out where the best part of the fairway is to get you there. Tee the ball up and use the club that will put you in that position. Play for the position, not the distance.

4 Sometimes tee markers are misaligned, pushing you into the rough or the trees not down the fairway. Take the left-hand marker out of your mind by teeing close to the right – so you can see it from the corner of your eye. Then imagine the left marker is in the correct position before making a positive swing.

Coping with pressure

Jack Nicklaus

Country USA

Born 21 January 1940

Notable achievements
Open Championship winner 1966, 1970, 1978; US Masters winner 1963, 1965, 1966, 1972, 1975, 1986; US Open winner 1962, 1967, 1972, 1980; US PGA winner 1963, 1971, 1973, 1975, 1980; Ryder Cup 1969, 1971, 1973, 1975, 1977, 1981, (captain) 1983, (captain) 1987

Jack Nicklaus is one of the greatest golfers ever to have played the game. He dominated major championships throughout the 1960s and 1970s, winning 18 and coming second a further 19 times. He was the first power golfer, hitting long and straight, and also had enormous powers of concentration as well as a ruthless competitive streak. In his early years, he stole the crown as king of the sport from Arnold Palmer, and their rivalry in the first part of Jack's career was one of sport's enduring battles. With Gary Player, the threesome took the sport from minor interest to global commercial entity. Jack's legacy stretches beyond his major achievements. Where Arnold brought glamour and excitement, Jack brought steely competition, power and an unquenchable thirst for success – his last major triumph was in the US Masters in 1986, aged 46.

How to follow Jack's pre-shot routine

Jack Nicklaus' approach to golf was underpinned by an unnerving ability under pressure. This was because of his reliance on a solid and simple pre-shot routine. Because it never changed, his body always knew what it was doing. The importance of a pre-shot routine cannot be over-estimated. It pre-sets the body for success.

1 Before every shot, stand behind the ball and visualize its flight; see it curve in the air and drop to wherever you want. Jack's powers of imagination set him apart, and he never played a shot until he had built a clear mental picture of what he wanted to do.

2 Track an imaginary line from the target to a point a metre in front of your ball – it is simpler to align yourself with something close than something 185 m (200 yds) away. This clear point can be a daisy, an old divot or a mark in the grass, but must be in line with your ball and target.

Jack Nicklaus stood on the 18th tee in a play-off for the 1970 Open Championship. He needed to beat Doug Sanders, who the day before had missed a 1 m (3 ft) putt and so the chance to win the title. This error had resulted in the play-off. Unperturbed, Jack took off his sweater, ran through his routine and smashed the ball to victory on the 18th green.

Pro tip

Use your pre-shot routine in practice. Run through your routine every time you play a shot so it becomes second nature to your swing. By the time you finish your practice session, it should feel strange to make any stroke without running through those simple steps. Never waste a session by blasting a bucket of balls quickly.

3 Set the clubhead behind the ball, aligning it with this point. Make a few practice swings to get a feel for the shot prior to this alignment. For Jack, the crucial point was that his clubhead had to point at the target before he would align his body, shoulders and feet.

4 Jack would then make the same amount of waggles as usual and swing. The routine needs to take the same time for each shot. The pre-shot routine is a familiar and faithful cocoon to disappear into when you are under pressure. Always keep it the same.

On-course tactics

Despite all the power hitting and tenacity under pressure, the greatest strength of Jack Nicklaus' game was his on-course tactical ability. Commentators of the day said that Jack may have played bad shots but he never made the wrong one. His intent was always perfect.

Jack Nicklaus

Country USA

Born 21 January 1940

Notable achievements
Open Championship winner 1966, 1970, 1978; US Masters winner 1963, 1965, 1966, 1972, 1975, 1986; US Open winner 1962, 1967, 1972, 1980; US PGA winner 1963, 1971, 1973, 1975, 1980; Ryder Cup 1969, 1971, 1973, 1975, 1977, 1981, (captain) 1983, (captain) 1987

Jack Nicklaus played in six Ryder Cup teams as well as captaining the side in 1983 and 1987; he only ever lost three matches. One of the most enduring images of that event is Jack conceding Tony Jacklin's short putt on the 18th green in 1969, which left the overall score of the match tied. The pair left the green with arms around each other's shoulders. As his career wound down, Jack played regularly on the Seniors Tours, winning ten times including eight Seniors majors. He finally retired from competitive golf in 2005 after an emotional appearance at the Open Championship at St Andrews, the scene of two of his Open titles. Jack is still a major figure in the golfing world, whether endorsing a new product, overseeing a course-build or being free and easy with a quote and opinion.

How to decide your on-course tactics

Jack Nicklaus excelled at both game-plan tactics and technical tactics. He won more majors through mind power than muscle power, and his opponents knew this. He had such a psychological hold over his own game, the course and the other golfers that they regularly played for second place.

1 Create a picture as your last thought before moving the club. In your mind's eye see the shape of the shot, the trajectory and result, as well as feeling it. Jack extends this to technique. 'If I think of swinging slowly, my last thought isn't "swing slowly". It is an image of me swinging slowly.'

2 Use one club extra when you are approaching the green, whether it is your second shot or a tee shot on a par three. Don't use the club that will get there with a perfect strike. At his best, Nicklaus reckons he hits three or four perfect shots a round. This means you are unlikely to strike all of your iron shots perfectly.

3 To cope with water or out-of-bounds, aim at the trouble spot and work the ball away; or aim away from it and work the ball towards it. Jack decides on his tactic by thinking about how he has been playing. If you are playing well, hit at the trouble and fade the ball away, otherwise, hit away from the trouble completely.

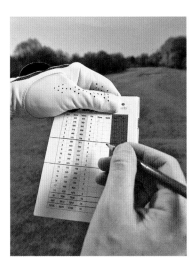

4 To deal successfully with a strokeplay round, divide it up into manageable bites – three six-hole courses, for example – and set yourself targets for each section. This will make it easier to forget disasters and not get carried away with a run of good holes. To manage yourself round the course, you have to be able to divorce yourself from the situation and play each shot on its own – in isolation.

Pro tip
If you are ever caught between two clubs, select the shorter iron and make an aggressive swing. If you take the longer club and swing easy, you are likely to hesitate and decelerate in your swing, leading to a poor strike. This is a great rule of thumb to stick with and applies to most situations. Always bear in mind the best place to miss.

Fairway woods and long irons

When Tiger Woods won the 2000 Open Championship at St Andrews, he became only the fifth and youngest player to win all four majors. The outstanding shot in a tournament in which he did not go in a bunker was a 265 m (290 yds) fairway wood on the par-five 14th during his third round. This set up a birdie. In achieving this shot, Tiger displayed his solid technique combined with nerve and pure athleticism.

Tiger Woods

Country USA

Born 30 December 1975

Notable achievements
Open Championship winner 2000, 2005, 2006; US Masters winner 1997, 2001, 2002, 2005; US Open winner 2000, 2002; US PGA winner 1999, 2000, 2006; Ryder Cup 1997, 1999, 2002, 2004

Tiger Woods had won ten major golf titles by his 30th birthday – a record unsurpassed even by the great Jack Nicklaus. The expectation for Tiger to dominate is now so great that a season such as 2003, where he collected five titles and won the money list on the US PGA Tour, was reported as a slump. He bases his game around extraordinary power born from a superhuman flexibility married to awesome strength. Tiger has an outrageously sharp short game as well as iron nerves under pressure, particularly when faced with a 3 m (10 ft) putt. Overall, he has raised the bar in professional golf, and the rest of the world is still struggling to catch up.

How to play a fairway shot

Tiger Woods' power helps him score well on par fives. Much of this is because of his ability with fairway woods, where he is confident and aggressive, sometimes even hitting a driver off the fairway to chase up those extra metres. Tiger says that the setup for the fairway wood is much the same as for his driver.

1 Place the ball forward in your stance, almost opposite your left heel, and angle your spine slightly away from the target to ensure that you will stay behind the ball throughout a powerful swing. If you are playing a driver, aim left of the target as the ball is likely to fade to the right.

2 Take the club back low to the ground, and slowly, to play a good fairway-wood or long-iron shot. Width in the swing is one of Tiger's key thoughts, and then making sure he completes his backswing, turning his shoulders as much as he can manage so his back faces the target.

3 Make sure the bottom of your swing is where the ball is. Solid contact is the key to unlocking the power in your swing, according to Tiger. Try to extend your arms fully through impact so that you sweep the ball off the turf at the lowest point of your swing rather than hitting down at it.

4 Swing a long iron and fairway wood with confidence, as if they are short irons. By swinging a 3-iron like a 7-iron, you will naturally let the extra shaft length and setup alterations sweep the ball cleanly off the surface, without taking a divot. You will not need to swing hard or try to help the ball in the air.

Pro tip

If you are struggling with your long irons or fairway woods, try adding a rescue club to your bag. These are hybrid clubs, half wood and half iron, which are simple to use from the rough or fairway, and will give you the distance of a longer iron, while maintaining the control of the shorter iron.

Successful short irons

In 1999 Greg Norman, Davis Love III and José Maria Olazábal were playing the back nine on the final day of the US Masters. When Davis, playing in the group ahead of José Maria, improbably chipped in for birdie on the par-three 16th, the crowd were screaming for a home victory. José Maria held his nerve and hit a peerless iron to 1.2 m (4 ft), holed the putt and retained his two-shot lead, to claim his second major and his second Masters.

José Maria Olazábal

Country Spain

Born 5 February 1966

Notable achievements
US Masters winner 1994, 1999;
Ryder Cup 1987, 1989, 1991, 1993, 1997, 1999

José Maria Olazábal had overcome severe adversity in the years before that win in the 1999 US Masters. In 1995 he had had to withdraw from the Ryder Cup, because of painful feet. Soon he could not even get out of bed. José Maria was eventually treated by a German doctor, who rediagnosed the problem as rheumatoid polyarthritis in both feet, treated it and had him back playing golf within 18 months. Two years later José Maria won his second major. This majestic iron player formed the most successful Ryder Cup partnership with Seve Ballesteros, winning 11 matches, halving two and losing two. He has won 22 European Tour titles since turning professional in 1985. José Maria has always been a popular player, with ragged driving, great escape shots and a sensational putting touch.

How to play irons accurately

José Maria Olazábal's famous short-iron play is a result of a tight-controlled swing, with minimal lower-body movement, and a vicious downward blow into the back of the ball. Mimicking this will improve your short-iron consistency. José Maria fights against a reverse weight transfer which, on the short irons, might help but is best avoided in general.

1 Take your normal posture and place a club behind your shoulders while holding on to both ends; then flex your knees. This and the next step form a drill José Maria uses to battle with reverse pivot, when his weight goes the wrong way slightly as he swings, onto his left on the way back, then onto his right through impact.

2 Coil your upper body around your spine so the club turns over 90 degrees (or as far as you can manage) and points towards your right toe. Make sure your weight is on your right side in this position, which is a good strong one for the top of your backswing. If you have kept flex in your right knee, your weight should automatically be on your right.

Towel tuck

Take a bag towel and secure it under your right arm. Then hit practice balls, holding the towel in place as you swing and only letting it drop at impact. This forces you to keep your arms close to your body, helping the connection between upper and lower body.

The ball squeeze

Place a ball underneath your right heel, squeezed into the ground slightly so it does not roll, then twist your ankle. Make swings with the ball in place. This drill will force you to flex that right knee and maintain your spine angle throughout, as well as improve your weight transfer through the ball.

Pro tip

Find out how far you hit each iron. Go to the range, warm up, and then hit 20 balls with each club. Ignore the best and worst five shots with a club, then average out the distance you hit the remaining ten. Do this for every club in your bag. Use this knowledge on the course and don't think: 'I can get there with a 7-iron if I really hit it.' Use a 6-iron.

Fairway
tactics

It may not have been the most important tournament of the year but the manner of Jim Furyk's 2005 Nedbank Challenge victory summed up his game. A bogey at the last hole, when a par would have won, left him in a three-way tie with Darren Clarke and Adam Scott. Jim regained his composure, and on the second play-off hole he chipped in for a birdie and victory. Clever management won him the event.

Jim Furyk

Country USA

Born 12 May 1970

Notable achievements
US Open winner 2003; Ryder Cup 1997, 1999, 2002, 2004

Jim Furyk is not the most glamorous of golfers in America but is among the most successful. His steady approach and good course tactics have established him firmly in the top-ten ranked golfers in the world, and were it not for injury through the 2004 season he would be pushing the top five. Jim has a swing you don't forget: a round-the-houses twirl at the top that leads to a powerful drive through impact. With such a technique, though, Jim does not possess the range of shots of other top players, so he relies on dogged determination and grinding it out. He has won nine times on the US PGA Tour and is a constant threat at events where the scoring is high; he had 12 top-ten finishes in majors before he won the US Open in 2003. He hangs in there, either outlasting his opponents or forcing a race down the back nine on the final day.

How to adopt better fairway tactics

Jim Furyk's clever strategies and knowledge of his own game make him a difficult opponent. He plays within himself, makes sure his bad shots are not that poor, and he benefits when others make mistakes. Here are four top tips for better preparation and management.

1 Keep the ball in play. If the ball is in play, you can make a score – at worst a bogey. Jim will play conservatively off the tee, and lay up if he feels that is the safest option. The result is that he maintains his rhythm and composure because he never smashes the ball into the stream and gets cross with himself.

2 To regain composure after either a birdie or a double-bogey, play a confidence club from the next tee, even if it gives you a longer approach. This will give you a chance to find a calming level. Jim copes well with swings in fortune, and not getting carried away with good shots is as important as coping with the poor holes.

3 Before you tee off, go to the practice range and play the first hole in your mind. Hit the club you intend to hit from the tee, then follow it up with the likely second. Repeat this process so you hit the course running. A good start means you are chasing a good score rather than recovering from early damage.

4 If you are in the rough and thinking of playing a big-hero shot, think how many times out of ten you are likely to pull it off. Is it more than seven? If so, it might be worth having a go. If it is fewer than seven, put the 5-wood back in the bag and knock the ball to safety. This simple rule will help you prevent bad situations becoming disastrous.

Pro tip
Professional golfers reckon they can shave at least five shots off any mid-handicapper's score through careful shot selection and simple course management, and without changing their swing. It is worth having a playing lesson with your local pro and taking advice on the correct shots to play. You will learn all about the mistakes you have made.

Pitching
basics

Tom Lehman's rich form and good showing in the biggest tournaments through the middle of the 1990s earned him the world No. 1 spot for one week only. This solid US PGA Tour pro forced himself into this slot through hard work and a simple repeatable technique. He won the 1996 Open Championship at Royal Lytham, in England, and to win around any such links course you have to control the ball well from 90 m (100 yds) and in, which was the deciding factor in his one and only major triumph.

Tom Lehman

Country USA

Born 7 March 1959

Notable achievements
Open Championship winner 1996; Ryder Cup 1995, 1997, 1999, (captain) 2006

Tom Lehman spent a number of years learning how to win, earning his playing rights via the satellite tours in the United States, and was clearly doing something right in the lead up to the 1996 Open Championship. He had played in the final pairings of the US Masters in 1994 and the US Open in 1995 and 1996. Tom has battled hard at keeping his simple, unique swing consistent and repetitive, yet has won only five US PGA Tour events (including that major triumph). He is a proud Christian, has put much of his success and consistency on Tour down to his marriage, and he is generally regarded as one of the laid-back golfers on Tour. Tom was chosen as captain of the United States 2006 Ryder Cup team.

How to develop good pitching

A simple, repetitive swing requires simple, repetitive basics, and this is what Lehman brings to the course and what makes him so strong from 90 m (100 yds) and closer. He can 'feel' from this distance, because his easy pitching style involves hardly any movement in his body.

1 Aim left of the target at address, giving yourself room to swing your arms through the ball but keeping the clubface aimed directly at the target. Maintain a good, solid posture, with your back straight and some gentle flex in your knees. You should be loose and flexible, not rigid.

2 Hover the club off the ground before playing, or gently rest it on the turf. As a result you will have to hold the club gently, which can only improve your feel for the shot. It will also help to release tension.

3 Play the ball back in your stance, so it is near your right foot. You should hit down on the ball, taking the ball first and turf second. Let your hands rest forwards, ahead of the ball; they should remain ahead of the club through the swing. Stand with your feet about a shoulder's width apart, to reduce lower-body movement.

4 A common mistake is to address a pitch shot in a similar manner to a full shot with your feet too wide holding a club at the end of the grip. If you play like this, you will lose feel for the stroke and use too much lower body, which could lead to a deceleration towards impact. So don't align parallel to the target and do have your feet closer together

Pro tip

Choke down the club when you are pitching for added feel and control. Use your orthodox (reverse-overlap) grip and hold it gently, trying to feel the distance in the shot. Play with natural flair and instinct from 90 m (100 yds) and closer, by emptying your mind and simply picturing the ball flying the right distance and finishing close.

Pitching swing

Darren Clarke is one of the biggest modern names in European golf and is the only European to win a WGC (World Golf Championship) event – the minor majors. As a result of learning the game on Northern Ireland's links courses, Darren has a compact efficient swing and is particularly deadly from 90 m (100 yds) and closer.

Darren Clarke

Country Northern Ireland

Born 14 August 1968

Notable achievements
Ryder Cup 1997, 1999, 2002, 2004

Darren Clarke is a fast-living, aggressive golfer who enjoys a few cigars during his rounds as well as laughs and jokes with his playing partner. He is enormously talented, and it is surprising that he has not clinched a major title yet, despite coming close on a number of occasions. His most memorable achievement was winning the WGC Accenture Matchplay event in 2000, beating Tiger Woods in the final, and he became the only person other than Woods to win a second WGC event, when he claimed the 2003 NEC Invitational. Darren was also the first European to shoot 60 for a second time, at the 1999 European Open; previously he had scored 60 at the 1992 European Monte Carlo Open. Despite his undoubted talent and ball-striking ability, Darren has won only nine titles on the European Tour and a few overseas ones.

How to play the perfect pitch shot

The reason Darren Clarke is the one to watch when it comes to learning how to pitch is the simplicity of his swing. He has few moving parts and relies on his shoulders and hands to punch aggressively through the ball, keeping it low and controlled into the wind with great control and spin.

1 Take up a good address position with your feet closer together than normal. Then choke down the grip, so you will be in good shape for making a solid swing from your arms and shoulders only. Keep your lower body still and stable. Correct adjustments at address make this easier to do.

2 To make an aggressive back-and-through motion, take the club back with your arms and rotate your upper body so that your back faces the target. Keep tempo consistent and use your length of backswing to control the shot. Work out how far you pitch for different backswings, so you can adopt the correct shot when needed.

3 From this solid position on the way back, drop the club into the back of the ball, using minimal lower body movement. Imagine you are rotating through the ball, from a position with your back to the target to one where you are facing the target. Make sure you accelerate into the back of the ball, and be aggressive through impact.

4 Finish with your hands the same distance in your throughswing as they were on the way back. If you swung to waist high on your backswing, stop with your hands at waist height in the finish position. Think to finish in this good position to help you make a positive strike and accelerate through impact to avoid mishits.

Pro tip
Go to the range and practise pitching with a variety of clubs. More lofted clubs will fly higher and give you less run, whereas a longer club may be the best option when pitching into a stiff breeze. Practise controlling the ball's flight and distance, by mixing and matching your club selection. You will discover a number of useful shots.

Escaping from the rough

Arnold Palmer

Country USA

Born 10 September 1929

Notable achievements
US Masters winner 1958, 1960, 1962, 1964; Open Championship winner 1961, 1962; US Open winner 1960; Ryder Cup 1961, (captain) 1963, 1965, 1967, 1971, 1973, (non-playing captain) 1975

Arnold Palmer played golf with the same energy that he uses to attack life. The first major won by this charismatic and exciting player was the 1958 US Masters – a tournament that became his own at the beginning of the 1960s. He won 92 professional tournaments including 62 on the US PGA Tour. His most spectacular win was in the 1960 US Open, where he overhauled a seven-shot deficit at Cherry Hills in Denver. While Arnold was in his prime, he and his business manager Mark McCormack set up organizations and deals around the world, from course design to aviation, that still make Arnold one of the highest-paid sportsmen on the planet. Arnold is renowned as one of the friendliest faces in golf, with time for every fan and businessman.

How to get out of the rough

Arnold Palmer was a ferocious striker of the ball, which is a useful attribute when you are trying to escape the thick stuff. Strong wrists and forearms will help you chop through the entangling grass, just as they helped Arnold. He advises golfers to avoid over-ambitious shots. There is no point playing a fairway wood or long iron from the rough.

1 Address the ball opposite your right heel. Have your feet further apart than normal, to help stability. Then choke down the grip of your mid-iron (at longest) slightly.

2 Pick the club up slightly more steeply than you would normally, to avoid snagging the grass on the backswing and to encourage a steep approach towards impact. Otherwise the swing is basically the same as your normal swing, because you don't want to veer too far from your fundamental technique.

Arnold Palmer was the first golfing superstar – enormous armies of fans supported his every round. He played with passion, style and aggression, but this would occasionally land him in trouble. Arnold escaping difficult situations or blasting balls onto the green from claggy rough therefore became a common sight.

Pro tip

Be realistic with your ambitions. Your priority is to get onto the fairway or in a manageable position in no more than one shot. If you take on the hero shot, it could end up costing you plenty more than if you had laid up. Remember Jim Furyk's strength – keeping the ball in play at all costs (see page 57).

3 Watch closely the exact spot where you are hoping to strike the ball. You are looking to chop hard down at the back of it, with that steep approach swing. Power is key here. Drive the clubhead to the bottom of the ball so you can dig it out of trouble.

4 Try to swing as far through as you can, although driving through rough may truncate your finish. Also move less weight onto your right side and instead try to feel that you are pushing directly down strongly with your right leg towards impact. This will help you drive the clubhead through the entangling rough.

Fairway bunker shot

Sandy Lyle

Country Scotland

Born 9 February 1958

Notable achievements
Open Championship winner 1985;
US Masters winner 1988; Ryder Cup
1979, 1981, 1983, 1985, 1987

Sandy Lyle is one of the European 'Big Five' who challenged America's status as the world's dominant golfing power in the 1970s and 1980s. He was coached by his father, was blessed with enormous natural ball-striking ability, and came of age at Royal St George's in 1985, where he won the Open Championship – the first Briton to do so since Tony Jacklin in 1969. The tall Scot also won the US Masters in 1988 in memorable fashion,

birdying the last. Since 2000, Sandy has had a resurgence with a number of top-ten finishes in both regular tour events and major championships. He has always been a down-to-earth golfer, not one of the most glamorous figures on the professional circuit. Sandy has also been a key member of five Ryder Cup sides, winning in 1985 and 1987.

How to play the perfect fairway bunker shot

Sandy Lyle's famous ball-striking ability was essential when playing his wondrous shot under the most extreme pressure at the 1988 US Masters. He was able to make a completely clean contact with the ball and to drop the ball close to the flag because he was arguably the best golfer in the world at that time. You should not be too ambitious with this shot.

1 The setup is key to playing this shot effectively. Use a club that has enough loft to clear the lip of the bunker. Select one longer club than you would normally use from that distance on the fairway. Place the ball forward in your stance and grip the club more tightly. Don't shuffle your feet into the sand as you would for a greenside bunker shot.

2 As you take the club back, keep your lower body as still and balanced as possible. Don't worry if you use a truncated backswing – the extra club will make up for a shorter swing. It is essential to keep your balance and ensure a pure strike. Your setup changes encourage this.

In 1988 Sandy Lyle stunned the world by winning the US Masters thanks to an astonishing fairway bunker shot. At the time he was in a titanic struggle with Mark Calcavecchia and needed to birdie the 18th to clinch the green jacket. When his drive found the fairway bunker, all looked lost. But Sandy's clean ball-striking saved him: he hit his 7-iron to within 3 m (10 ft), sank the putt and claimed his second major title.

3 Accelerate the swing through the shot. You must go for a full aggressive impact, and not hesitate in the swing. Avoid taking any sand. You need all the energy of the club to go into the back of the ball, and not the sand.

4 Make as full and natural a follow-through as possible. The ball may take a shallower arc than you would normally expect from the club you chose, but the extra distance gained will compensate for this.

Pro tip
Grip the club tightly. This is the only time in golf when this advice is valid. By holding the club firmly, you shorten the distance from clubhead to your arms, which means you are more likely to catch the ball first and the sand second.

Damage limitation

Nick Faldo

Country England

Born 18 July 1957

Notable achievements
Open Championship winner 1987, 1990, 1992; US Masters winner 1989,1990, 1996; Ryder Cup 1977, 1979, 1981, 1983, 1985, 1987, 1989, 1991, 1993, 1995, 1997

As he approaches Senior golf, Nick Faldo has become a mentor for many talented and emerging European professionals – most notably Nick Dougherty, an exciting English prospect. He has developed many off-course businesses including course design, coaching academies, restaurants and vineyards, as well as hosting the Faldo Junior Series competition – an annual tournament for the best young players in Great Britain and Ireland. With his eye off the practice range, it is no surprise that Nick's golf has suffered, although he does achieve the occasional memorable event such as the 2003 Open Championship at Royal St George's, England, where he finished tied eighth, four shots behind Ben Curtis. He will always remain an iconic British golfing figure, and has a chequered relationship with the press but an ever-adoring public.

How to minimize your bad shots

Think about every hole on the course that you are about to play, picture each shot and where, if you have to miss, would be the best place to miss. These damage-limitation tactics can make all the difference over 18 holes as you can improve your percentage of greenside saves by leaving simple chips.

1 Readjust your game plan to make bogey your worst score and don't be afraid to make it. There is no point chasing birdies after a wayward drive. Accept that you will take an extra shot, chip out sideways and sign for a five – not a seven or worse.

2 Miss on the right side of the green. Take a sensible line to a flag that is tucked to one side of the green, behind a bunker, to avoid leaving a tricky next shot. Hitting to the heart of the green or away from the flag is often sensible; you don't want to be left with a tight bunker shot and no green to work with. You are better playing a longer chip.

At the top level of professional golf, all the players can regularly hit the ball close from 90 m (100 yds) and sink the putt. But it is the players whose bad shots are less bad than those of the rest who make the most money. Nick Faldo won the 1987 Open Championship because no one could match his 18 straight pars and he did not make mistakes, or the errors he made were not as bad as his opponents' ones.

Pro tip

Set yourself a realistic target of greens in regulation, then keep stretching them and forcing your game upwards, but don't become too obsessed with playing perfect golf. Remember the best golfers in the world will hit only 13 greens in regulation on an average round, so if you are missing a few you are in good company.

3 Pick a less ambitious line if you have cut off too much fairway on a dogleg, or are in the rough trying to escape. If you have to hit a tree with your rescue shot, make it the last tree. Your ball will go nowhere if you clatter into the nearest branches, but you may have a chance if you pick out the last in line!

4 When you are laying up, play the club that will definitely avoid trouble, even if it means you are 18 m (20 yds) back. Give your swing room to breathe by taking a shorter club, concentrating on the shot as hard as you would an approach, and by swinging positively down the target line.

Adverse weather conditions

If you are to become one of the Open Championship's greatest winners you must be able to play in all types of weather. Tom Watson won five Opens, including the famous 'duel in the sun' with Jack Nicklaus in 1977 at Turnberry. But his ability to score when conditions were tough marked him out as a truly great links golfer.

Tom Watson

Country USA

Born 4 September 1949

Notable achievements
Open Championship winner 1975, 1977, 1980, 1982, 1983;
US Masters winner 1977, 1981;
US Open winner 1982; Ryder Cup 1977, 1981, 1983, 1989, (non-playing captain) 1993

Tom Watson is one of the all-time greats, and he is still picking up cash regularly on the Seniors Tours. Tom started his golfing career in 1971 after he completed a psychology degree at Stanford University, California. Four years later, at the Open Championship at a blustery Carnoustie, in Scotland, he sank a 6 m (20 ft) birdie putt on the 72nd hole to force a play-off against Australian Jack Newton, which he won. Through the end of the 1970s and early 1980s, Tom's flared trousers and cloth cap embodied the image of the Open Championship and, despite putting problems later in his career, he remained competitive at the highest level beyond the age of 50. When Jack Nicklaus retired from competitive golf at the 2005 Open Championship, Tom accompanied him – a fitting tribute to two of golf's greatest rivals. Tom made the cut and played all four rounds.

How to play in the wind

Tom Watson's ability to use the wind around links courses and cope with nature led him to being the most successful Open Champion in modern times. Keeping the ball under control in a stiff breeze is essential on seaside courses. Here are a few tips to avoid being blown off course.

Playing into the wind

1 Set up with the ball back in your stance, feet closer together than usual and take a longer club than you would play from a similar distance in still conditions. Also, choke down the grip for added control. The key when playing into the wind is not to try and hit the ball hard.

2 Make an easy swing at the ball with a shortened backswing and full follow-through. It is essential that you have a full finish, to make sure you accelerate positively through the ball at impact. Keep your swing and tempo as even and as normal as possible.

Pro tip
Use the wind; don't fight it. Golf is a game best played as simply as possible. If there is a breeze off the right, aim further right and let the wind take your ball back on line; don't try to hold the ball up against it with a fade.

Playing with the wind

1 Off the tee, try to use the wind to your advantage and gain metres, so tee the ball high and play a more lofted wood – a shot from a 3-wood will fly further downwind than one from your driver as it flies higher.

2 With the ball forward in your stance and your feet wider apart, to give you added stability in windy conditions, make a full-long swing, maintaining your natural rhythm throughout. Apart from the slight setup adjustments, you should not need to make any alterations to your normal technique – just concentrate on making a pure strike.

Draw shot

During the 1980s and 1990s, if not leading in a major then Greg Norman was moving up the leaderboard. He had awesome power and a great range of shots that enabled him to score when others struggled, as he showed in the 1986 Open at Turnberry, by shooting a second-round 63 in windy conditions, finally winning the event by five.

Greg Norman

Country Australia

Born 10 February 1955

Notable achievements
Open Championship winner 1986, 1993, runner-up 1989; US Masters runner-up 1986, 1987, 1996; US Open runner-up 1984, 1995; US PGA runner-up 1986, 1993

Greg Norman is an exciting, powerful golfer who can shoot scores in conditions and on courses when others falter. He spent 331 weeks as the world No. 1 and won 20 US PGA Tour titles as well as 68 other wins around the world. His first major came in the 1986 Open Championship, in a year where he led after the third round of every major. He famously lost out to Bob Tway's holed bunker shot in the 1986 US PGA, and in the following year an unknown journeyman, Larry Mize, holed an outrageous chip in the play-off for the US Masters, to deny Greg the green jacket once again. But his defining loss was at the hands of Nick Faldo, who in the 1996 US Masters overcame Greg's six-stroke lead at the start of the final day.

How to play Greg's draw shots

Greg Norman achieved his successes because of his control. He hit the ball straight and far. But he could play all the shots in the bag, when the situation called for it. 'When I do work the ball, I keep the method simple, making no changes to grip or swing, I set up fades and draws entirely with my alignment at address,' admitted Greg.

1 Make the adjustments at address, not in the swing, if you want to play a draw. Work out where you want to start the ball – the point you want it to turn from.

2 Aim your body right of the target on the line you want your ball to begin but keep your clubface pointing at the target or where you want the ball to finish. These are simple changes and everything else at address should remain the same, including your grip, stance and posture. Change as little as possible.

3 Adopt these adjustments to encourage a takeaway that is more along the ball-to-target line than usual, resulting in an in-to-out hit. Your club approaches impact from nearer your body, putting draw spin on the ball and making it curve from right to left. Other than the changes at address, swing as normally as you can.

4 To control the amount of turn, alter the size of your adjustments at address. The more right-to-left movement you need, the further right you should align yourself, always keeping the clubface pointing at the target. A draw will always travel further than a fade or straight shot, so take one club less when playing this shot.

Pro tip

A draw can be a useful shot to play in a number of situations: for example, if you want to curl the ball round a dogleg, or gain extra metres off the tee. Also, if a pin is tucked behind a bunker to the left of the green, you can work the ball close from the right with a draw, without having to fly the ball over the hazard, risking dropped shots.

Fade
shot

Lee Trevino's distinctive yet controlled ball flight proved irresistible on links courses, especially at the 1972 Open Championship at Muirfield, in Scotland, when his victory over Tony Jacklin was one of the all-time great battles. Lee's chip-in on the 17th sunk Tony and meant that Lee successfully defended the title, to the dismay of the passionate British crowd.

Lee
Trevino

Country USA

Born 1 December 1939

Notable achievements
Open Championship winner 1971, 1972; US Open winner 1968, 1971; US PGA winner 1974, 1984

Lee Trevino grew up in a poor area of Dallas, in Texas, in a house that backed onto a golf course. He would pick up pocket money by caddying and hustling rich members out of cash, which prepared him for the pressures of professional golf. He once said: 'Pressure is playing for ten dollars when you do not have a dime in your pocket.' He turned professional in 1966 and won his first title and major in 1968, the US Open, becoming an instant star. Lee would chatter his way round the course, which endeared him to fans. Strangely, though, his patter was as a result of nerves, and off the course Lee prefers a more introverted and quiet existence. Having won four Senior majors, he retired from tournament golf in 2004, so he could spend more time with his family.

How to play Lee's fade shot

Thanks to his self-taught technique, Trevino hit the ball from left to right throughout his career, missing few fairways and greens. 'You can talk to a fade, but those hooks do not listen,' he once explained. His suggestion that a fade is easier to control than a draw is true. Johnny Miller said he would hit a fade by picturing Lee's swing and setup, then mimicking it.

1 Make sure you take an extra club when playing a fade, because the cut spin you put on the ball takes distance off the shot. Also, the less loft the club has, the easier it is to move from left to right.

2 Align your body well left of the target, looking to start the ball down the left and watch it drift into the middle of the fairway.

3 Aim your club where you want the ball to finish. Once you have made these simple setup adjustments, your swing will naturally cut across the ball from outside to in, putting left-to-right spin on it. The more you want to fade the ball, the bigger the adjustments you need to make to your address position and body alignment.

4 Swing as normally as possible and make sure you make a full swing. Any hesitation in the stroke could lead to a pull direct left, which is the opposite of what you are trying to achieve.

Pro tip

Many of the world's best players have a natural shot shape that they know they can repeat and are comfortable with. Lee's was a fade, as are Jack Nicklaus' and Colin Montgomerie's. Find your natural shape and use it to your advantage, starting the ball down one side of the fairway and letting it straighten to the middle.

Chipping
basics

Jesper Parnevik's solid performances in the Open Championship throughout the 1990s, and especially at the 1994 Open, made him a household name – and you cannot do well at the Open without a consistent short game. Much like Nick Price who defeated him in that 1994 Open, Jesper has a quick swinging tempo, which mirrors his exciting style of golf.

Jesper Parnevik

Country Sweden

Born 7 March 1965

Notable achievements
Open Championship runner-up 1994, 1997; Ryder Cup 1997, 1999, 2002

Jesper Parnevik is one of the most recognizable players in golf, with his famous upturned cap, distinctive bright outfits and his marvellous shot-making ability. He is one of the more colourful characters on the US PGA Tour, which he has played most of his career, picking up five titles amid making a lot of money and friends. His father Bo is one of Sweden's leading comedians and that eccentric edge has rubbed off on Jesper, who has a

devoted and crazy fan base. He is also famous for eating volcanic dust as a dietary supplement and lights a victory cigar whenever he wins. Jesper introduced Tiger Woods to Elin Nordegren, who was his children's nanny, who later became Tiger's wife.

How to play a chip shot

Like many of Sweden's best golfers who have grown up with solid coaching, Jesper Parnevik's basics are perfect and give him the chance to use his imagination and feel around the greens when the time calls for it. By keeping it simple, he rarely makes mistakes, especially under pressure. Simplicity is the key in chipping.

1 Hold the club as you would hold it for a full shot, but choke down the handle, so your hands are nearer the metal of the shaft. This gives more control and feel for what is a delicate touch shot.

2 Play with your feet close together and knees slightly bent so you are comfortable, flexible and solid over the ball. You don't want to be stiff and compromise your feel. By having your feet close together, you will swing with your arms and shoulders, keeping your lower body still, essential in consistent chipping.

3 Play with the ball back in your stance and your hands forwards. This will help you hit down on the ball. You want to make contact in the down part of the swing, hitting ball first then turf, which will give you more control and spin when it lands on the putting surface. Look to keep your hands ahead of the clubface throughout.

4 Keep the tempo of the stroke the same for every chip, accelerating through impact. Lengthen and shorten your backswing depending on distance, and keep your left wrist firm throughout. At impact, look to return to your address position, with no movement of your legs or lower body. This is an upper-body shot.

Pro tip
Go to the practice green and practise chipping with all your clubs – including woods – and you will develop a shot for every situation. Jesper's imaginative golf helps him make good scores and carve out birdie chances. He uses every club in his bag to get the ball close.

The chip-and-run

John Daly

Country USA

Born 28 April 1966

Notable achievements
Open Championship winner 1995;
US PGA winner 1991

John Daly is one of the most controversial and exciting figures in world golf. He came to recognition when he won the 1991 PGA Championship. He had made the field as ninth reserve, yet he overpowered the world's best players with his exciting swing and huge hitting. However, he is notorious for his hit-and-miss form: he is capable of shooting seriously high numbers, but if he is playing well then no one can touch him. When on form, he has an immaculate short game and great control on the greens to add to his enormous length off the tee. That is why he is such a crowd puller – you never know what you are going to get. This characterful golfer has battled with alcohol and wives; he has been poor and rich; and he has released a record (one of the songs is called 'All my exes wear Rolexes').

How to play a chip-and-run shot

John Daly's Open win in 1995 was carved out of a solid short game under pressure, where he was able to keep the ball under the wind and under control around the vast greens of St Andrews. His lightness of touch and rhythm when playing a chip-and-run set him apart. He is a master at picking the right moment to play this shot.

1 Position the ball back in your stance – opposite your right foot with your hands forward.

2 Keep your hands forward of the clubhead throughout the stroke, maintain the same rhythm as for your other shots and just use the length of your backswing to dictate how far the ball travels – the farther you take it back, the longer the chip. You are looking to chip the ball low so it flies a few metres over the fringe of the green before rolling.

Although John Daly is famed for an extravagant swing and long hitting, it was his control on and around the greens that won him the 1995 Open Championship, at St Andrews. His chipping and imagination were put to the test on the Old Course, and thanks to an unchallengeable touch he defeated Costantino Rocca in a play-off, to claim his second major.

Pro tip
To gauge how hard you should hit the shot, stand behind the ball, look at the shot you are playing and imagine rolling balls underarm at the hole. The club is just an extension of your arms, so when you are playing the shot use that same feel to hit the right distance.

3 Drive the clubhead positively through the ball at impact, keeping your hands loose and gently holding the club so you can feel the shot; try not to hesitate or tense at impact. For such a big and aggressive golfer, John's feel is remarkable; he holds the club gently and strokes his chip shots with great rhythm and artistry.

4 Ensure your hands are ahead of the ball at and beyond impact and keep the clubface heading towards the target. Just let the loft on the clubface do all the work; there is no need to use your wrists and manufacture height on the shot. Keep your body steady and still throughout and use only your shoulders, rocking them back and forth, to play this shot.

Flop shot

How to play the perfect flop shot

If you have to chip over a bunker to a flag that is close to the edge of the green, you need to stop the ball quickly once it lands, as Phil Mickelson did at the 2005 US PGA. You cannot let the ball run up to the hole as you have no green to work with. When faced with such a scenario, you should use the flop shot, provided the lie of the ball is suitable.

1 Select your most lofted club from the bag. Align your body left of the target with the clubface pointing where you want the ball to finish. This setup position is similar to a greenside bunker setup (see pages 86–87).

2 Make a full backswing along the line of your body. Take the club back along the line of your body; don't align it with the target. This should happen naturally thanks to the adjustments in your setup.

Phil Mickelson is famed for his exciting golf and in particular his aggressive and imaginative short game. When faced with a 18 m (20 ft) chip over slopes or bunkers, Phil lofts the ball high in the air, stopping it dead where it lands. This is a high-risk shot, but when it comes off it is dramatic and extremely effective. In 2005, for example, he used his trademark short-club flop shot to set up a birdie on the final hole at Baltusrol, to claim the US PGA title.

Pro tip

Open the clubface first and then take your grip. If you do this the other way round, you will produce a closed face at impact, the opposite of what you are trying to achieve. Try not to be too scientific about the shot but 'feel' the distance, like Phil, and let the artist in you take over by using your natural touch.

3 In your downswing and through impact, you are looking to swing across the target line – this opens the clubface and adds loft to an already lofted club. At impact, the ball will pop upwards, with less forward momentum. As with all short-game shots, accelerating through the ball at impact is vital.

4 The swing should be aggressive, so have a full flourish in your finish position. Any hesitation in this shot will result in a thinned shot scooting through the green or a duff one that leaves the ball a metre in front of you. If the shot is successful the ball will loop high in the air and drop dead next to the flag, leaving a short putt.

Playing the bellied wedge

Mickelson's flop shot is not the only showy, short-game technique you can adopt to impress your playing partners. Try this useful way to rescue your ball from a difficult spot. If your ball nestles between the fringe of the green and the rough, it is tricky to get a clean strike with an orthodox chip, so don't worry about a clean strike. Take your wedge and use its leading edge to strike the ball deliberately around its equator, so you are not trying to loft it in the air. Play the shot like a putt, with your putting stroke and grip, and nudge the ball down the green with this intentional thin. Your partners will think you have made a mistake until they have to concede the putt.

Using your
imagination

Seve Ballesteros' short game was legendary. He had the ability to get the ball close from any situation, however difficult, using his astonishing imagination and skill. There were so many times when he seemed sunk but conjured remarkable escapes that his legacy is one of shooting low numbers without ever hitting a fairway.

Seve
Ballesteros

Country Spain

Born 9 April 1957

Notable achievements
Open Championship winner 1979, 1984, 1988; US Masters winner 1980, 1983; Ryder Cup 1979, 1983, 1985, 1987, 1989, 1991, 1993, 1995, (captain) 1997

In 1976 a dashing 19-year-old playing swashbuckling, daring golf just lost out to Johnny Miller in the Open Championship. From this moment on, Seve Ballesteros was a star. He won the 1979 Open Championship at Royal Lytham with amazing putting and rescue shots – including a famous escape from a car park – and then added two US Masters titles and two more Open Championships to his major collection. Arthritis in his back eventually took its toll and his driving suffered badly, forcing him away from competitive golf for years. He is remembered for his imagination and range of shots that, at times, defied belief. As long as Seve could get his club to the back of the ball, he could get it close.

How to invent good chip shots

Seve Ballesteros was not only born with a genius golfing mind but he also nurtured it. He would play rounds with only one club to develop a variety of shots for any situation. He might also throw balls into difficult places to see if he could escape. Here are four ways to develop your creativity.

1 Work your way back from the hole to whatever position you are in. Seve would always try to land the ball on the flattest part of green he could manage. This would cut out any inconsistent and unpredictable bounces. You will have a better idea of how the ball will move on the flat parts of the green than on a slope.

2 To develop an idea of how balls react in various situations, take a bucket of balls and throw them at the hole. Lob some high in the air; roll others along the ground. Then use the contours and levels on the green to hit the ball close to the hole. You will be surprised at the variety of ways you can chip a ball.

3 Practise chipping from one place, but try the same shot with a variety of clubs in your bag. Don't be afraid to have a go playing a lob shot with a 3-iron. Seve would spend hours manufacturing and manipulating shots from a variety of positions with a range of clubs, just so he would be covered for any situation he encountered.

4 Make your practices fun, laugh at what is impossible, then try it. Put a bit of Seve into your practice. This most charismatic golfer of his generation played with a smile on his face, a twinkle in his eye and joy in his swing. He had fun playing and practising – it loosened his mind, allowed him to think the unthinkable and try the impossible.

Pro tip

Seve's top tip for developing imagination is to practise with only one ball. This makes you take every shot seriously and treat it for real. You also learn more from its reaction on the green, because you are concentrating solely on that ball, and not getting ready to hit the next one.

Rescue-club chip shot

In 2004, Todd Hamilton won the Open Championship using his rescue club to chip-and-run the ball across the quick links turf. His killer moment came during the play-off with Ernie Els, when Todd recovered from a wayward drive to scramble a title-winning par by chipping dead with his hybrid 3-wood.

Todd Hamilton

Country USA

Born 18 October 1965

Notable achievements
Open Championship winner 2004

Todd Hamilton had been earning a decent living playing golf, winning 11 times on the Japan Tour, before he finally secured his card on the US PGA Tour in 2003, after failing eight times at US qualifying school. He plays a steady conservative game, hitting fairways, finding greens and taking his chances when they come while not making any mistakes. His experiences in Japan have taught him how to compete and how to win, and this was

evident as he ground down Ernie Els on the final afternoon of the 2004 Open Championship. When all expected Todd to fade under pressure, he stuck to his simple game, never trying to compete with more illustrious names off the tee or on approaches. He just concentrated on his own score, which was a lesson to every golfer watching the match.

How to chip with a 3-wood or rescue club

Playing a chip shot with either of these clubs is a risk-free option once you have practised. Todd Hamilton had played a number of practice rounds on fast-running links, working out the best situations in which to use this tool. Chipping with a 3-wood or rescue club is best done on tight turf or out of fringe grass where your clubhead might snag.

1 Hold the club down the grip and use an orthodox (reverse-overlap) putting grip.

2 Play the ball back in your stance, opposite your right foot. You are looking to roll the ball along the ground with only a short hop just after impact. Using a putting grip should make you instinctively take up a putting posture, key for this technique.

3 Rock the club back and through, using your shoulders while keeping your lower body still and steady. This should be similar to your putting stroke. Let the weight of the clubhead create the momentum in the ball; don't add any energy by flicking your wrists or swaying your legs into impact. Try to keep the head of the club low.

4 Use the length of your backswing to judge distance and maintain your rhythm, accelerating through impact. This shot does require practice to gauge how far a particular length of stroke travels, so pay a visit to the range and find out how versatile your 3-wood or rescue club can actually be in a number of situations.

Pro tip

A rescue-club chip shot is especially useful on parched courses off bare lies, as it gives greater margin for error than using a sharp-edged wedge. Find a piece of hard ground, take an old rescue club and practise off this surface. You will have to be accurate with your technique and ball striking to play this shot successfully.

Chipping on the green

Sergio Garcia is blessed with golfing intelligence and a magical touch around the greens, which many professionals lack. During the second round of the 2003 US Masters, for example, Sergio was faced with the same chip back down the green on the 18th hole as Padraig Harrington, who had earlier dribbled the ball 18 m (20 ft) past. Garcia hit it so close to the hole that the putt was unmissable.

Using the chip putt

One way to control delicate chips, especially downhill or when you are tight to the putting surface with not much green to work with, is to play the chip-putt shot. This has the control of a putter but the loft of a wedge. Take a 6-iron or 7-iron but hold it as you would your putter, and address the ball as if preparing for a putt. Then make a putting stroke, rocking with your shoulders only, so the ball pops up over any fringe grass and starts rolling quickly; don't use any wrist hinge. The ball will never come off the face as fast as with a normal chipping stroke.

How to play a delicate chip shot

Sergio Garcia's chip in the 2003 US Masters was remarkable not so much for its execution as for its conception. The ability to see how to play that shot was what made it so good. You can practise your vision and imagination when playing chip shots; it is not necessarily a god-given talent.

1 Land the ball on the flattest part of the green as quickly as possible and get it rolling. This is a basic rule of short-game golf. There is no point floating a ball high in the air over a flat green to land it close by the hole. You would have to judge height and distance, as well as being at the mercy of the elements.

2 Play for the break; do not just chip at the hole. You may always read the break on the green when you putt, but golfers often forget to read the break when they chip. This is why Sergio's chip was so masterful; he judged the slope and break to perfection, letting the ball feed to the hole.

3 Try to hole every chip shot. If you do try to sink each chip, you will swing more positively, make a cleaner contact and, you never know, you might actually sink a few. When putting, you would always try to hole out, yet golfers will play chips from a similar distance and erroneously not think to hole the shot.

4 Imagine the putt back. Give yourself a chance for the return putt. That is the minimum you should aim for from a chip. If you do not manage to hole out, then you should leave yourself close, and below the hole with an uphill putt. Also, pay attention to the break as the ball passes the hole, as this is the route the ball will take on its way back. This is a putt you have to hole.

Pro tip

When you are planning an approach shot, work out where the best place around the green is to play a recovery chip, if you have to miss. It will be the spot that leaves the most green between your ball and the pin. This will give you plenty of green to work with when chipping, and so improve your chances of getting the ball close to the hole.

Bunker basics

Ernie Els

Country South Africa

Born 17 October 1969

Notable achievements
Open Championship winner 2002;
US Open winner 1994, 1997

Ernie Els is one of those astonishingly talented individuals who could have been a professional – and probably world champion – at a number of sports. Although a good cricketer, rugby and tennis player, he chose golf. His easy swing and relaxed attitude tell nothing of the fiery competitor within. Ernie has won only three majors to date but is in contention in virtually every one he plays. In any other era, he would have dominated world golf.

As it is, this easy-swinging, pure-striking South African has lived in the shadow of Tiger Woods for much of his career. He has won the World Matchplay title at Wentworth a record six times, as well as the European Order of Merit in 2003 and 2004, which was a notable achievement considering how much he plays around the world. This global golfing hero has amassed a vast fortune through prize money and endorsements.

How to play a greenside bunker shot

Ernie Els' remarkable bunker escape at the 2002 Open Championship was a result of his reliance on solid basics. Although his feet were in a strange position, he did not over-complicate the shot, but kept his setup and swing as close to normal as possible.

1 Hold the club correctly: to play a decent bunker shot with a sand-wedge, you need to open the clubface. However, it is essential that you open the clubface first, then take hold of the club. If you do this the other way round, the clubface will shut at impact, which is the opposite effect to the one you want and you will have no control.

2 Set up to the ball with the clubface square to the target but with your body aligned left of the hole. This is what Els was able to do in his bunker shot: he opened up his body to the target and then swung down the line of his body. This position makes best use of the sand-wedge.

While chasing his first Open title round Muirfield in 2002, Ernie Els found a nasty spot up against the lip of one of the deep, steep bunkers on the par-three 13th. His recovery with one leg up the bank, the other in the sand, is the stuff of legend. Ernie not only got the ball out in one, but was unlucky for the ball not to drop for a two. He later won the tournament in a play-off – thanks to another wondrous sand save.

Pro tip

If you are trying to blast out of a bunker, don't ground your club before playing the stroke; if you do, you will suffer a one-shot penalty. Such a penalty applies to any hazard, so don't let your club get wet too early when trying to play out of water, or use the club as a support when clambering round the edge of a stream.

3 Shuffle your feet into the sand to give yourself as stable a base as possible. Such a position also lowers the swing arc – the plane that the clubhead swings in – which makes it easier to hit the sand first and the ball second.

4 Play the ball forward in your stance, so you are more likely to catch the sand first, and tilt your spine slightly away from the target, keeping your knees gently flexed and back straight. This is a good, solid but flexible position, which is important when you are standing on a slippery, sandy surface.

The bunker swing

Gary Player, one of golf's greatest heroes, is regarded as the best bunker player of all time. He once said: 'If I am one of the greats, it is for one simple reason: no bunker shot has ever scared me and none ever will. Approach every bunker shot with the feeling you are going to hole it.' Frequently, he managed to achieve just that.

Gary Player

Country South Africa

Born 1 November 1935

Notable achievements
Open Championship winner 1959, 1968, 1974; US Masters winner 1961, 1974, 1978; US Open winner 1965; US PGA winner 1962, 1972

In many respects, Gary Player was one of the first modern golfers. He was the first professional to place an emphasis on fitness and strength, and his work ethic was staggering. His never-say-die attitude won many admirers as well as a fair few tournaments. With Arnold Palmer and Jack Nicklaus, Gary dominated the golf world through the 1960s into the 1970s, picking up nine major championships and becoming one of only five people to have won every major title. He was well known for his on-course patter, and wound up countless opponents through a combination of his chat and obstinate competitiveness. When he reached 50, in 1985, he became a dominant Seniors player. Gary is also a successful businessman off the course, using his high profile to good effect in course-building, coaching academies, running a stud farm and countless other ventures.

How to develop a good bunker swing

Gary Player practised hard at retaining his reliable bunker technique. He kept the basics as well as the swing simple, and then worked on a repeatable, solid movement that made him relish the challenge of the sand, and not dread it. He would prefer to be in a bunker than chipping from the fringe, as he knew exactly how the ball would react.

1 Build a good stance and address position, with the clubface open and your body aligned left of the flag. Maintain that good posture, with straight spine and flexed knees. Such good core stability was something Gary's fitness regimes helped him with.

2 Imagine there is a line in the sand drawn along your feet. You want to take the club back along this line, then swing back down along it towards impact so you are cutting across the ball-to-target line with an open clubface.

3 The open face and the design of the sand-wedge mean your club will bounce through the sand, taking a scoop with it. Take the sand from underneath the ball so that the ball floats out of the hazard on a cushion of sand. You don't want to make any direct contact between clubface and ball.

4 Control the distance out of the bunker by shortening or lengthening your backswing, depending on how far you want to hit. Always hit the sand a consistent distance behind the ball – about 5 cm (2 in) – whatever the shot. You have to catch sand first, or you will have no control.

Pro tip

Aim for the top of the flagstick when you are in a bunker. By aiming high, you are more likely to hit beyond the hole and give the ball a chance of dropping into the hole. Most amateur golfers leave the ball short, which gives it no chance of dropping at all.

Bunker tactics

Tony Jacklin's Open Championship win in 1969 was remarkable for its steadiness. But what kept his score down to a winning 72 were his powers of recovery. 'When I won the Open, I found a lot of sand during the final round – I counted 11 bunkers. But I got up-and-down out of every one of them.' Tony became the first Briton to win that title in 18 years.

Tony Jacklin

Country England

Born 7 July 1944

Notable achievements
Open Championship winner 1969; US Open winner 1970; Ryder Cup 1967, 1969, 1971, 1973, 1975, 1977, 1979; (non-playing captain) 1983, 1985, 1987, 1989

Tony Jacklin was the first European golfer of the modern era to make headway in major tournaments dominated by the Americans. He is one of only three Britons to win the US Open, his victory coming 50 years after Ted Ray gained this title in 1920. This son of a Scunthorpe lorry driver displayed prodigious talent from an early age, before turning professional and making a mark on the US PGA Tour, where he played most of his tournament golf. Perhaps Tony's greatest achievement was in creating a competitive Ryder Cup. His (non-playing) captaincy produced victorious Ryder Cup sides in 1985 and 1987, which were the catalyst to the vast interest in the competition nowadays. Tony was on the receiving end of one of the great sporting moments of the 20th century, when Jack Nicklaus conceded a putt to halve the 1969 Ryder Cup.

How to play bunkers like Tony

The reason Tony Jacklin could escape so consistently from a bunker was not only because of his solid technique and good practice but also because of his mindset when in the sand. He had honed decent bunker tactics, which gave him the best possible chance of getting up-and-down. The golden rule of bunker play is to escape the trap in one shot.

1 Look to give yourself a chance with the shot once you are out of the bunker. The ball does not have to drop dead next to the hole, as long as you have an opportunity to get close or sink it.

2 The conditions of the sand dictate how you should play the shot. Shuffle your feet into the sand to get a feel for the texture. If it is deep and fluffy, you may need to open your stance more to swing to the bottom of the ball. If the sand is hard or wet, your best option might be to play an orthodox pitch or chip (see pages 58–59 and 74–75).

3 Using a lob-wedge can be a good option instead of a sand-wedge, because the ball will not fly as far and so it gives you an opportunity to swing positively. If your ball is buried, then a pitching wedge or sharper-edged club is the right tool to help you dig the ball out of the bunker in one positive blow.

4 Check the lie of the bunker. If you are hitting from an upslope, the ball will fly higher and not as far, so aim to take slightly less sand. If you are on a downslope, take more sand with your swing. Look to chase the ball down the slope to make sure you escape immediately.

Pro tip

If you can relish the challenge of escaping from bunkers, you will play more aggressively and make fewer mistakes. Once you have developed good technique, you will realize that there is more margin for error when escaping from bunkers than anywhere else on the golf course.

Popular types of putting grip

Because Fred Couples is one of the most rhythmic, attractive players in the world, his putting is often overlooked. However, only a year after he changed his grip from an orthodox (reverse-overlap) to a cross-handed grip, he won the 1992 US Masters with a solid and sometimes brilliant putting display. Such a grip change is a big deal to a top player, but it made all the difference to his game.

Fred Couples

Country USA

Born 3 October 1959

Notable achievements
US Masters winner 1992; Ryder Cup 1989, 1991, 1993, 1995, 1997

Fred Couples is a former world No. 1 who was one of the dominant players in regular Tour golf at the beginning of the 1990s, yet he has only one major to his name. He has, however, enjoyed success in other big events on both sides of the Atlantic, winning back-to-back titles on the European Tour in 1995 as well as the Players Championship twice. If it were not for a bad back, Fred's reign as the world's leading player might have been longer.

He was a regular member of the US Ryder Cup side through the 1990s, and found a resurgence in form at the start of the new century, winning consistent cash when other players from his era were being swept aside by Vijay Singh and Tiger Woods. When Fred graduates to the Seniors Tour, he will make a fortune.

How to understand Fred's grip changes

Fred Couples used two types of putting grip in his career: the orthodox (reverse-overlap) grip, and the cross-handed grip. Each has its advantages, and different players are comfortable with each type. A cross-handed grip is a great way to rejuvenate your stroke. Tweaking your technique can refresh your feel, as it did for Fred.

Orthodox putting grip

1 Put your left hand on the club as you would for a normal full swing (see pages 22–25). Let the grip run through the palm of your hand, and not the base of your fingers, helping to take the wrists out of the stroke. Lift the index finger free from the club, but keep it as close to your normal grip as possible.

2 Place your right hand on the club and let the index finger of your left hand rest on top of your right. Try to run the grip of the putter through the palm of your hand, as opposed to the base of the fingers again. Then move your hands together, so they are acting as one unit.

Pro tip

Chop and change freely between grips. Always do what is most comfortable. Your technique can get stale, which will numb your feel for the stroke, so tweaking your grip can reinvigorate your instincts and improve your touch. In putting, there is no correct grip.

Cross-handed putting grip

1 Put your right hand on the club, at the top of the grip with your palm facing the target. You are going to putt with your right hand above your left.

2 Place your left hand on the club, below the right hand, with the back of your left hand facing the target. With this grip, your shoulders become parallel with the ground, which makes it easier to swing the putter straight back and straight through, keeping the putterhead low to the ground throughout the stroke.

Less common putting grips

Bernhard Langer suffered from the yips, which is essentially a phobia of short putts. This debilitating putting condition reduces even the best players in the world to 18-handicap amateurs. Bernhard's solution was to change his grip completely and rebuild his game, and he subsequently gained another US Masters title, in 1993.

Bernhard Langer

Country Germany

Born 27 August 1957

Notable achievements
US Masters winner 1985, 1993;
Ryder Cup 1981, 1983, 1985,
1987, 1989, 1991, 1993, 1995,
1997, 2002, (captain) 2004

Bernhard Langer is one of Europe's 'Big Five' golfers. Alongside Nick Faldo, Ian Woosnam, Sandy Lyle and Seve Ballesteros, Bernhard has been responsible for establishing European players in the modern game and the European team in the Ryder Cup. Through meticulous organization and planning, he out-thought the American team when European captain during the 2004 Ryder Cup. Bernhard was the first No. 1 ranked player in the world when the ratings were launched in 1986, and he remains a force on both Tours over 20 years later. He is the only German golfer to win a major championship and is almost solely responsible for his country's love of the game. For a player who bases his game round on-course control, accuracy and preparation, he has an unusual twirl and flourish in his follow-through that is more pronounced the closer he is to winning.

How to understand Bernhard's putting woes

For all Bernhard Langer's control and preparation, there was nothing he could do about an attack of the yips. This affliction makes short putts impossible, because the player loses control of the putterhead and flicks involuntarily at the ball. Bernhard's solution was first a new grip, then when the yips recurred he tried a new putter – the increasingly popular broomhandle one.

Bernhard's yips-curing grip

1 Place your left hand on the putter shaft just below the grip, where the rubber meets the metal. Let the rubber of the grip run up the inside of your left forearm so the forearm and putter are pinned together as one.

2 Bring your right hand onto the top of the grip and use your right thumb to hold the left forearm and putter's grip steady and together. What this method does is take the wrists completely out of the stroke. You putt with shoulders and forearms alone, so you cannot involuntarily flick at the ball.

Broomhandle putter grip

Place the end of the putter in your sternum and hold it with your left hand, so that your watch face is pointing directly away from you. Make a stroke with a rocking motion, holding your wrists and shoulders on the line parallel to the ball-to-target line.

Claw grip

Hold the top of the putter in your left hand, thumb pointing upwards, with the back of the hand facing the target. Bring your right hand below this, palm facing the target and hold the club with a claw-like grip. Your left hand holds the putter steady, while the right guides the stroke.

Pro tip

If you are struggling with the yips, try putting left-handed if you are a right-handed player, and right-handed if you are a left-handed golfer. By using the same muscles in a different fashion – backwards – you can rediscover your touch. Buy a two-faced putter, one that you can use either way round, and play whichever way feels best.

Putting posture

Paul Casey is one of the newest English golfers to make his mark both in the USA and Europe. His game is distinct due to its athletic strength and power, which come from hard work in the gym. Paul has one of the most solid techniques, especially when it comes to his putting stroke, where his posture and basics provide great reliability.

Paul Casey

Country England

Born 21 July 1977

Notable achievements
Ryder Cup 2004

Paul Casey is a burgeoning talent. He may not yet have gained that major breakthrough but he has won regularly on the European Tour and has experienced great success in a variety of team events, including playing a crucial role in the 2004 Ryder Cup victory. When Paul turned professional, he already had a rich amateur career behind him. He won four matches from four in the 1999 Walker Cup, claimed the English Amateur title in 1999 and 2000 and broke scoring records set by Tiger Woods and Phil Mickelson while at university in the United States. His game is well suited to the US Masters, and he came sixth in his debut in 2004. With a powerful long game and sharp putting technique, Paul looks set to become an exciting fixture on world leaderboards over the next decade.

How to build good putting posture

The importance of correct posture when putting cannot be over-estimated. If you have a good, comfortable stance, your stroke will withstand the pressures of competition. Paul Casey is a young, strong golfer who looks incredibly stable when standing over a putt.

1 Stand upright with the ball in your normal putting position and your feet a shoulder's width apart. Have your putter resting on your side so you can easily take hold of it. Make sure your back is straight. Lift your chin up, let your arms dangle naturally by your sides and stay relaxed.

2 Bend from your hips, creating an angle between your upper and lower body. Keep your back and your knees straight, and let your hands dangle naturally down from your shoulders. Keep your chin up and shuffle until you feel comfortable, ensuring that you remain relaxed.

3 Flex your knees and look down at the ball. Keep your hands in that natural position directly under your shoulders. The ball should be underneath your nose. Keep your back as straight as you can but make sure you are comfortable – comfort is the most important element of putting, because this is where you can develop good feel.

4 Take hold of your putter, which should now rest naturally behind the ball. When you bring your hands together, the putter, posture and stability are all in the correct place. If you practise achieving good posture, your putting stroke will become more consistent.

Pro tip
The correct position for the ball is essential for good posture. It should be directly under the bridge of your nose. If you were to drop a ball from your nose when you are in your address position, it should land on top of the ball on the ground. Adjust your address stance so that the ball position is accurate and comfortable.

Putting stroke
principles

Among the best putters is Ben Crenshaw, who has won two US Masters titles with superb displays of control around the greens. During his 1995 win Ben did not three-putt once, and this was mostly because he possesses the most enviable putting stroke in golf.

Ben Crenshaw

Country USA

Born 11 January 1952

Notable achievements
US Masters winner 1984, 1995; Ryder Cup 1981, 1983, 1987, 1995, (captain) 1999

Ben Crenshaw is among America's greatest players, especially on the greens, although he never backed up his undoubted talent with all-round major success. Having been mentored by legendary golf coach Harvey Penick, Ben's proudest moment was his 1995 US Masters triumph one week after the funeral of his teacher. He captained the US Ryder Cup side to victory in 1999, engineering the biggest rearguard action that event has seen. Ben has always been a firm believer in fate, saying before that famous fightback on the final day of the Ryder Cup that he 'had a good feeling'. Similarly, his 1995 Masters win was put down to Penick's divine spirit being the 15th club in his bag. He is known as Gentle Ben, initially ironically because of a lively temper, then sympathetically when he became an elder statesman in the game.

How to imitate Ben's putting stroke

Ben Crenshaw has the most natural and consistent putting stroke. He has struggled to explain the secrets himself but the most important factor for him has been comfort. As long as he was relaxed over the ball, everything else would fit into place. By using his big, reliable muscles such as his shoulders, Ben was able to putt well under pressure.

1 Stand tall to the ball; don't crouch over it hurting your back. The ball should be forward in your stance, with your hands slightly ahead at address. Hold the putter very gently and in a relaxed way so that you can feel the putt. Don't strangle the grip with tension.

2 Hold the putter with two thumbs on top of the grip and with your hands parallel to each other. This is a natural position and makes it simple to line the putterface square to the target at address. Open your stance slightly, for added comfort, and then just think about pace and line.

3 Make a natural, slow stroke, with a beautiful rhythm to it and pivoting from the shoulders only; there should be no wrist action in the stroke.

4 Always look to putt at the right pace, so the ball stops just by the hole. Ben explained: 'The ball which arrives at the hole with the proper speed has an infinitely greater chance of falling in the hole from any entrance. Harvey Penick taught me the value of this method at an early age. This is what he meant by "giving luck a chance".'

Pro tip
A simple drill to help develop a smooth, comfortable stroke that is not too bogged down in technique is to make putts with only your right hand. Enjoy the freedom, natural rhythm and comfortable posture such a technique develops. Then replicate this when you address a putt for real. You will soon rediscover a flow in your stroke.

Putting stroke for the orthodox grip

The best modern-day putter is universally regarded as Brad Faxon. He may have won only eight times on the US PGA Tour, yet some of his statistics are mind-boggling. In 2003 he went 19 rounds – that is a total of 362 holes – on the Tour without three-putting. He is a consistent top-ten performer despite the odd wild drive and few tournament wins.

Brad Faxon

Country USA

Born 1 August 1961

Notable achievements
Ryder Cup 1995, 1997

Brad Faxon's first win on the US PGA Tour came in 1991, and he has picked up tournaments regularly since then. This quality competitive golfer also tops the putting statistics most years. If you are putting well, it gives the rest of your game some leeway, and this has translated into a lot of prize money for Brad. He works closely with Dr Bob Rotella to keep his mind in tune, retaining a simple game and playing to his strengths. He rarely leaves a putt short, because he always tries to hole every putt. However, Brad is never too disappointed if the ball slides past. This has always been his great strength, giving himself a chance to score well but not berating himself if it does not work out.

How to use the orthodox (reverse-overlap) putting stroke

Brad Faxon does not believe there is a right or a wrong way to putt. He has seen too many good putters with all manner of techniques. So it is ironic that his stroke is pure orthodoxy and simplicity in itself. He uses an orthodox (reverse-overlap) grip, concentrates on line and strokes, and empties his mind.

1 Focus your eyes so they are on an imaginary line slightly closer to your body than the line of the putt, and hold the putter gently. These straightforward solid fundamentals should be copied by any amateur, particularly those struggling with pace.

2 Just before you take the putter back, make a barely perceptible forward press with your wrists. This is a trigger movement – it lets the rest of your body know that preparation is over and the real thing is about to start. It is an easy and natural way of starting your stroke and can be used for a full swing as well as putting strokes.

3 Ensure your stroke comes from your shoulders and keep your wrists and elbows very still, but not locked or stiff. Your wrists and elbows should be soft and comfortable in the stroke; there should be no tension. This method gives great feel and touch throughout, as well as maintaining rhythm and tempo.

4 As you take the club back, open the clubface slightly so the putter moves in a gentle inside-out swing path. This is what works for Brad. Many players prefer a straight-back, straight-through stroke, or an inside-to-inside one – like a swinging door; both are equally effective. As long as your stroke is consistently repeatable and delivers the clubhead square to the ball at impact, it does not matter what path the putter takes.

Pro tip

Brad believes that the most important element in putting is your mind. If this is clear of doubt and clutter, you will putt positively and well. Pick a line and stroke the ball down that line – it is as easy as that. The skill is in emptying your mind, and this is achieved on the practice green by honing your instincts and routine.

Long putts

In the 1999 Ryder Cup, the Americans were increasingly sensing victory during the course of the Sunday singles matches. Justin Leonard was playing José Maria Olazábal in the crucial game, and they both faced 45 m (50 ft) putts on the 17th green at Brookline. Justin sank his ball, while Olazábal missed (after an American stampede across his line). The American team therefore gained the vital point to reclaim the Ryder Cup.

Justin Leonard

Country USA

Born 15 June 1972

Notable achievements
Open Championship winner 1997;
Ryder Cup 1997, 1999

Justin Leonard is a hard-working, talented American golfer with an edge beyond that of a standard journeyman Tour professional. He is a great putter, as demonstrated by his huge effort at the Ryder Cup and in his 1997 Open Championship triumph. That Open win came as a result of mature golf stirringly displayed by a 25-year-old who held his nerve while chasing Jesper Parnevik's five-shot lead. Justin also played an important part in the extraordinary 1999 Open Championship at Carnoustie, when Jean van de Velde blew a three-shot lead on the last hole, forcing a play-off against Justin and the eventual winner, Paul Lawrie. The grit and grind of this stern competitor were also a driving force behind the 1999 Ryder Cup victory for the USA.

How to develop long-range putting skill

Becoming a solid putter from distance is about practice and touch. Justin Leonard's touch is one of the best in the world, and he spends hours doing putting drills. If balls are dropping into the hole for him, they tend to keep finding their target. Putting from a distance is all about pace. If you can roll the ball the right length, you will never be far from the hole.

1 Work on the feel and distance of the putt, but do not spend too much time reading the green's slopes. Of course, make a general read, but there is no need to work out the curves, bumps and turns for every millimetre of the putt's path.

2 Make practice strokes while looking at the hole. Stand behind the ball, so you can see it and the hole in the distance, then make practice swings trying to gauge the feel. Don't be too scientific, keep making strokes until it feels right, then take that feel over the ball and make the putt. Picture the correct speed of the putt in your mind.

3 All putts are straight putts. Pick a point in between the ball and the hole, and putt to that. Line yourself with that position and picture the ball rolling over that particular point before turning towards the hole. You cannot affect the putt once it leaves your putter; all you can do is make it roll over one specific spot at a good pace.

4 The length of your backswing, not the strength of your stroke, dictates how far you hit the ball. The longer the putt, the longer the backswing. Keep your rhythm and tempo consistent for all putts. The throughswing should be the same length as your backswing to ensure you hit positively and aggressively through the ball. Simply adjust the length of your backswing for the distance of the putt and roll it dead.

Pro tip
Always aim to leave the ball beyond the hole. This gives you a chance to read the break on the green for the putt back. Also, you may get lucky and the ball may drop in the hole; it will never go in if you leave it short of the hole.

Holing
clutch putts

Johnny Miller's 1976 Open Championship win at Royal Birkdale may be forever overshadowed by the emergence of a 19-year-old Spaniard called Seve Ballesteros. However, Johnny's outstanding final-round 66, including a rash of birdies and an eagle on the back nine, was the ultimate in performing under pressure and sinking clutch putts when it mattered. Although clutch putts tend to be 2–3 m (6–10 ft) from the hole, at a crucial moment in a match or tournament they are easily missed by even the best.

Johnny Miller

Country USA

Born 29 April 1947

Notable achievements
US Open winner 1973; Open Championship winner 1976; Ryder Cup 1975, 1981

Johnny Miller was an iconic golfing figure through the 1970s, with his flowing blond locks, chequered trousers and powerful technique. He is now a respected commentator on American golf, and he is not afraid to speak his mind. He usually gets away with it thanks to his successful playing career. Johnny won his first major, the 1973 US Open, with a record low score, and he claimed 24 titles on the US PGA Tour. He was one of the few players to challenge the dominance of Tom Watson and Jack Nicklaus through the 1970s and early 1980s, and he was the only person to break their monopoly on the money list between 1971 and 1980. Putting problems did, ultimately, lead to Johnny's retirement from competitive golf, although there was little wrong with his stroke during that 1976 Open Championship, his second major win.

How to putt under pressure

Pressure on the greens may ultimately have ended Johnny Miller's career, but his presence on the leaderboard in 1976 resulted from the way he coped with tension and achieved a low score in the toughest competitive conditions. Despite the mounting pressure, Johnny used a lipstick from his wife's handbag to sink those putts on that final day at the 1976 Open.

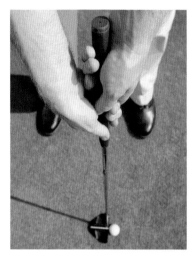

1 Place a red dot on the end of your putter. Keep your mind on the dot (not the ball) and maintain your tempo, while making your putt.

2 Treat each putt the same; use the same routine that you are comfortable and confident with, whether it is your first putt of the round or a putt on the 17th to take the match up the last hole. A classic amateur mistake when faced with a crucial putt is to over-analyse the situation. You don't want to increase pressure in your mind.

3 Always aim within the hole from 2.5 m (8 ft) and closer – especially on a clutch putt. Your instincts will force you to stroke more positively and you will increase your chances of holing out. When you are faced with a vital putt, you don't want to leave it short by aiming outside the hole – the ball will never go in.

4 Try to hole a hundred 1 m (3 ft) putts in succession. Tell yourself that you are not finishing until you have managed a hundred putts without missing. Go back to zero when you miss. You will soon feel the pressure as the sun drops and your stomach rumbles. This is a good drill to help you feel what it is like to hole putts under pressure.

Pro tip

If you are in a pressure situation, more often than not you are battling to win a match. If you are winning, remember that you must be playing well to be in this position in the first place, so make sure you enjoy it. Breathe deeply and hole everything. You are clearly in good form, so there is no excuse to miss any putts.

Reading
greens

Tom Kite won his only major at Pebble Beach in 1992 by shooting 72 when the average score for the day was 77. Many players failed to break 80 in the prevailing tough windy conditions. In such weather, putting becomes even more crucial, and a misread can cost dearly. Tom's steadiness was a marvellous example of control and clarity amid chaos.

Tom Kite

Country USA

Born 9 December 1949

Notable achievements
US Open winner 1992; Ryder Cup 1979, 1981, 1983, 1985, 1987, 1989, 1993, (captain) 1997

Tom Kite is among the most successful golfers of his generation even though he has only one major championship title to his name – and that was won later in his career. His US Open victory in 1992 was in the sternest conditions as he ousted Jeff Sluman and Colin Montgomerie with a steady 72. This prodigiously talented player won his first event aged 11, turned professional in 1973 and was Rookie of the Year. Tom has twice topped the money list on the US PGA Tour and has made seven Ryder Cup appearances as well as captaining the losing American team in 1997. Using his trademark thick specs, he has always battled with severe short-sightedness, but had laser eye surgery in 1998 to correct the condition. This has improved his on-course results, and he has won seven times on the Seniors Tour.

How to read greens

Because it can be difficult to read the best line for a putt on the green, Tom Kite worked with Dave Pelz – America's putting guru – to make it more simple and to explode some of the myths and learning tricks. Tom believes you can learn how to read a green. It is not a gift you were born with or without.

1 He realized that standing directly behind the ball to read the putt was inconsistent with what you are trying to do. If you are playing for the break on the green, then you will not putt the ball straight at the hole so why look at the hole in a straight line. This results in putting too straight and missing the hole on the low side.

2 Read the putt from the angle you want to start the ball rolling, then aim at one specific point on that angle. As soon as you start to do this, you will not be kidding yourself about the lack of break. Amateur golfers always under-read putts, which means the ball is breaking away from the hole at the end of its roll.

3 Check the position of physical features around the green. The sea can often give you a clue as to the break on the green: balls will, more often than not, break towards the sea and away from a mountain. The reason is simple physics: although the green may look flat, the overall lie of the land is always going to slope towards water.

4 Visualize the ball rolling towards the hole on your intended path before you putt; this will help you cope with pressure and clear your mind in tough conditions. Imagine the ball taking the break and then dropping into the hole. Then picture it coming out of the hole and rolling back to your putterhead. Your body will take these clear messages and naturally make them happen, ignoring all the competitive and windy distractions.

Pro tip

Remember that balls break different distances in varying conditions. If the green is fast and dry, there will be more break than if it is cold and wet. Uphill putts break less than downhill ones. Bear this in mind when you are reading a green and you will sink more putts.

Putting tactics

In order to win the US Masters, there is one element of your game that has to be working really well – your putting. Ian Woosnam negotiated the rolling ice-rink greens at Augusta better than anyone else when he claimed his only major title in 1991. The key to putting well on these greens is tactics: playing the correct shot in and then making the right putt.

Ian Woosnam

Country Wales

Born 2 March 1958

Notable achievements
US Masters winner 1991; Ryder Cup 1983, 1985, 1987, 1989, 1991, 1993, 1995, 1997, (captain) 2006

Ian Woosnam has been a stalwart on the European Tour for 26 consecutive seasons, winning 44 tournaments worldwide, and was one of Europe's big-five golfers when he won the 1991 US Masters. During the 1993 Ryder Cup, he was the only European to win all his foursomes and fourball matches. Although he is short, he is a ferociously powerful player with a good, solid short game. He has variously changed from a broomhandled putter to an orthodox one, yet his putting became hit-and-miss later in his career. Woosie is one of the European Tour's great characters, not particularly taken with workouts in the gym but more concerned with enjoying a drink after the game. He is also a good snooker player and is known to practise his putting on the snooker table. This ever-popular figure was European captain of the 2006 Ryder Cup side.

How to follow Woosnam's tactics on the green

Winning the US Masters is all about playing imaginative golf from tee to green, then clever golf once you are putting. Woosnam's triumph was a lesson in management and ball control on the putting surface. Here are a few tips to help you make the most of matchplay situations on the greens.

1 Think about the approach shot. You have to hit the ball to the correct side of the green to have the best chance of holing the putt. An uphill putt is always easier than a downhill one, so try to leave your ball below the hole. If in doubt, aim for the flattest part of the green, even if you feel it is farther away from the flag.

2 Use your opponent's ball as a clue as to how your putt might break and the pace of that particular green, especially if their putt is on a similar line to yours. Each green can differ slightly. Also, if you are playing a fourball match, help each other by planning to hit to similar parts of the green, giving you two chances at the same putt.

3 Keep your body still throughout the stroke. Most putts are missed through too much lower-body movement. Keep your lower body steady; then your stroke will remain steady and you will make the most of your preparation and read of the green. Don't jerk your head up too early to see where your ball has finished.

4 Lose count of your score. Don't add pressure to your game by thinking you have to hole this to break a personal best or keep your score going. Play each shot on its own, in isolation, worrying only about the challenges presented there and then. There are enough difficulties in putting without adding unnecessary pressure.

Pro tip
Bear in mind the weather conditions when judging the speed of a green. They can change pace, especially if it has been a sunny day. They can become faster as the dew dries in the morning, and then slow down as the sun bakes the surface to a crumbling crust.

Practice
routines

In 2003 the remarkable happened, Tiger Woods ceased to be the world No. 1 golfer. Vijay Singh usurped his title after a relentless winning streak that saw him clinch the 2003 and 2004 US PGA Tour money lists. The bedrock for this assault was Vijay's astonishing and relentless practice regime.

Vijay
Singh

Country Fiji

Born 22 February 1963

Notable achievements
US Masters winner 2000; US PGA winner 1998, 2004

Vijay Singh emerged as a club professional from the Pacific island of Fiji, playing on the Asian tours. He possesses great ability and has maximized his potential through hard work and graft. His single-minded attitude to practice and winning have not made him the most popular player on Tour. He enjoys his own company and can come across as surly. Vijay is a big-hitting, controlled player who sometimes experiences difficulties on the greens. If his putting is working he is uncatchable, but when he is having problems on the greens he returns to the realms of mortal golfers. In 2004 Vijay was only the sixth player ever to win nine US PGA Tour events in a season and earn more than a record $10 million.

How to develop a worthwhile practice regime

Vijay Singh is always trying to improve some aspect of his game. He practises before a round of golf as well as after it. At times, it seems as if the round were an inconvenient distraction between his practice sessions. Yet the more he practises the better he gets. Practising all the elements of your game is essential in improving quickly.

Make it count

Always have a purpose when hitting a ball down the range. Whether it is a technical drill, a discipline or a swing thought, there should always be one – and only one – thing going through your head. You would never hit a shot to nothing during a round, so why do this in practice?

Tailor-made practice

Set up a practice routine that suits you; don't force out unconstructive hours. Vijay spends hours practising, until he gets tired or bored. That is what works for him. Colin Montgomerie hardly practises at all, preferring to use the range as a warm-up. He has won eight European Orders of Merit.

Routine, routine, routine

One thing you can always drill, whatever aspect of your game you are working on, is your pre-shot routine, which will act as a cushion when you are under pressure. Every shot you play on the driving range will have a pre-shot routine, so it becomes second nature to you.

Practise putting

You use your putter on every hole, so make sure you spend hours drilling on the putting green, because this is where you can improve rapidly. It may not seem too exciting or fun, but there should be an even split between time spent on the green and on the range.

Pro tip

Have fun in practice. Golf is a hobby, a game and is supposed to be enjoyable. Go to the range with friends, have mini-contests and invent games in your mind if you are practising on your own. Stop if you get bored, because there is no point in working on your game if it triggers a dislike of the sport and technical destruction.

Practising on the range

Greg Norman

Country Australia

Born 10 February 1955

Notable achievements
Open Championship winner 1986, 1993, runner-up 1989; US Masters runner-up 1986, 1987, 1996; US Open runner-up 1984, 1995; US PGA runner-up 1986, 1993

Greg Norman earned millions of dollars through playing golf, but he now concentrates more on his financial ventures and boats than his golf. His Great White Shark enterprises includes golf-course design, bright clothing, wine, turf, restaurants, the internet – you name it, Greg has probably invested in it. He attacks his business ventures with the same energy he used to attack the practice range, which makes him a formidable moneymaker. Although Greg disappeared from top-level golf at the beginning of the 2000s, there is a sense that if he could be bothered he would have it in him to come back and compete as hard as ever. He did have a top-20 finish in the 2003 Open Championship, but typically now plays only a handful of events a season, maybe putting one round together but never maintaining the challenge.

How to practise like Greg on the range

According to Greg Norman: 'There is an old saying, "DIN and DIP" – Do It Now and Do It Properly. I am certainly not afraid to get my fingernails dirty and I am not afraid to go at a task myself and just get it done.' Here are four of Greg's best practice tips on the range.

1 'Start the swing with your left elbow', is one specific thought that Norman advises when working on the range. This ensures your arms and shoulders move away from the ball in one piece and that the club starts moving directly down the ball-to-target line. Working on such a simple thought is a good way to practise.

2 Think RPB – Right Pocket Back – especially when you are winding up for a big drive. This is a reminder to make a full backswing, turning the hips only half as far as the shoulders, which maximizes the coil in the swing and creates power. Practising with this thought adds metres off the tee.

Greg Norman was one of the hardest-working professionals on the circuit. Not only was he an enormously talented ball striker but he also spent hours practising to make the most of his ability. He may be remembered more for coming second but it was not through lack of trying that he came up short.

Pro tip

Practice does not make perfect; practice makes permanent. Before you go to the range, check that the specific technique you are working on is applicable and useful for your swing. If you drill the wrong thing, you will ingrain a faulty technique and play worse, despite hours spent on the range. It will also take longer to fix.

3 Vary the combination of clubs you use during your pre-round warm-up, working your way through half the clubs in your bag. One day, you might start with a sand-wedge, then 8-iron, then 6-iron. The next you could begin with a pitching wedge, 9-iron, 5-iron, and so on. As a result, you will favour all your clubs equally and not one over another.

4 Hit a bucket of balls on the range just after you have played a 18-hole round, because your body is warm and you can work on something specific that was not right during your round. Most golf professionals visit the range after a round of golf, and it is a good discipline for amateurs.

Best practice techniques

Ray Floyd has had a career of astonishing longevity. He is the only player to match Sam Snead's achievement of winning on the US PGA Tour in four decades, and with that experience comes knowledge. When Ray talks, golfers listen. To accomplish all this, he has had to spend hours on the range – perhaps more than any other player before him.

Ray Floyd

Country USA

Born 4 September 1942

Notable achievements
US Masters winner 1976; US Open winner 1986; US PGA winner 1969, 1982; Ryder Cup 1969, 1975, 1977, 1981, 1983, 1985, (non-playing captain) 1989, 1991, 1993

Ray Floyd has enjoyed one of the lengthiest careers in professional golf. He is the fourth youngest player to win on Tour, aged 20, and was the oldest player at the time to win the US Open, aged 43, in 1986. Ray has amassed 62 professional titles and is the only player to have won on the regular and Seniors Tour in the same season, 1992. He is also the only golfer to be selected from the Seniors Tour to play in the Ryder Cup (in 1993), four years after he was non-playing captain. Although Ray plays with a jerky and distinct loop at the top of his backswing, he has made the swing work to such great effect that he has picked up more than $17 million in prize money. Since cutting back on tournament golf in 2004, this ever-popular figure on Tour concentrates on golf-course design and endorsing an 'orthodic' shoe insert.

How to practise for longevity

Ray Floyd's experience in competition and preparation, and his unique swing, are useful when trying to learn how best to practise. His approach emphasized how important learning and amassing information from playing and practice are to becoming a decent player and making the most of your talents.

Play the best

Play against golfers who are better than you. 'I got dusted quite a bit in my early years on Tour,' said Ray, but each defeat was part of the learning process. By watching and learning from more experienced players, you will be assimilating that information and making it useful for your own game.

Play it safe

Develop a safety shot on the range, one that you know will keep you safe. Use it when the fairways look narrow and the trees thick, so you know you will keep the ball in play. Ray advocates this on-course weapon even though it is not the prettiest or longest shot, using a choked-down 3-wood or 4-iron.

Repeatable unbeatable

Ensure your swing action is repeatable and consistent. Ray's swing was distinct, natural and flowing. If a coach had tried to alter this method, Ray might never have earned any money on Tour. By being true to his talent and making it reliable, Ray's swing has stood the test of time, longer than that of any other player.

Longevity drill

Try hitting balls with your feet together. This quick drill helps your balance and ball striking, stops your lower body becoming too active and frees up your rhythm. Start with a 7-iron and see what is the longest club you can hit sweetly. Don't worry if you cannot do this immediately. It takes time to work out, but is a great drill once you have cracked it.

Pro tip

To make the most of your practice sessions, take a notepad and pencil to the range. Whenever you hit upon a good feeling or swing-thought that works for you, jot it down, what it felt like or what the thought was. Then practise these good, confident movements. Refer to your notes for a reminder if your technique starts to slip.

Putting practice

Sir Henry Cotton was the pre-eminent British golfer between the two world wars. He was renowned for his hard work on the range, often playing until his hands were raw and bleeding, and he also enjoyed the good life. He owned a country estate complete with a Rolls-Royce, a butler and other staff, and had a love of caviar, champagne and tailored clothes. Sir Henry brought an exciting flamboyance to the game, once saying: 'The best is always good enough for me.'

Sir Henry Cotton

Country England

Born 26 January 1907

Died 22 December 1987

Notable achievements
Open Championship winner 1934, 1937, 1948; Ryder Cup 1929, 1937, (captain) 1947, (non-playing captain) 1953

Sir Henry Cotton played mostly in Great Britain, winning three Open Championships, and competed in his last Open in 1977, 50 years after his first, in 1927. In 1937, he outplayed the entire American Ryder Cup team in the Open Championship (their presence being not too common in those days) to regain the title. He entered for only one US Open, because the Second World War coincided with his best years. In his later years Sir Henry wrote instructional books, designed courses and set up the Golf Foundation, a charitable organization that helps children take up the sport in the United Kingdom. He was awarded a knighthood a few days before his death in 1987.

How to tackle putting practice

Henry Cotton's intense practice regimes earned him respect as a professional and made him one of the best players in the country. Sir Henry once said: 'The big trick in putting is not method. The secret of putting is domination of the nerves.' Also, according to Sir Henry: 'Every shot counts. The 1 m (3 ft) putt is just as important as the 275 m (300 yd) drive.'

Gripping issue

Take deep breaths to lower your pulse rate before putting, if you are feeling under pressure on the green. Then make a conscious effort to lighten your grip on the putter. This will instantly ease the tension in your muscles.

Pressure practice

Practise putting under pressure. Place 12 balls around the hole about 60 cm (2 ft) away from it. Go round the circle of balls trying to sink each one. Once you have sunk them all in succession, move them back by 30 cm (1 ft). Every time you miss, start again; don't stop until you have made three moves.

Accelerate to dominate

Make sure that you accelerate through the ball for a short putt, making your follow-through double the length of your backswing. This will force you to speed up through impact, which means you can aim directly at the hole and don't have to worry about the break on the green unless it is severe.

Hear success

Keep your body completely still over short putts and listen for the ball rattling at the bottom of the cup – you will be amazed how many times you do hear that rattle. Don't watch the ball after you have stroked it. Most short putts are missed because you are too anxious to see where the ball has gone and so you move your lower body too quickly in the stroke.

Pro tip

Never expect a gimme (a conceded putt) and never accept one – a concession is supposed to be unmissable, so you will not have any problems holing out, will you? A gimme is a common practice in matchplay and can become tactical when opponents refuse to concede putts at opportune times. As a result, always hole out seriously.

Long putting practice

Byron Nelson

Country USA

Born 4 February 1912

Notable achievements
US Open winner 1939; US Masters winner 1937, 1942; US PGA 1940, 1945; Ryder Cup (non-playing captain) 1965

Byron Nelson is one of the game's all-time greats, even though he retired early, in 1955, due to health problems. These had also kept him from being sent to fight in the Second World War. During the 1940s, he earned prize money in all the 113 events he played, which meant a top-20 finish in every single one. He topped the US money list in 1944 and 1945, having won 11 consecutive events in 1945. Once he had retired from golf, Byron became a widely respected commentator, and even captained the Ryder Cup in 1965. Each year he hosts one of the biggest US PGA Tour events, the Byron Nelson Classic, and in 1993 he published *How I Played the Game*, his autobiography.

How to play consistently on the greens

Pace is everything over long putts – that is all you have to judge. Byron Nelson rarely made mistakes on or off the greens. To become consistent, you must aim to two-putt (at worst) every time you walk onto the green. Here are some tips when practising your pace putting.

1 Aim for certain areas of the green, marking each with a bag towel or tee pegs. Don't become overly concerned with the line of the putt. If your pace is accurate, then you will never be far from the hole. By having a larger target than just the hole, your feel will be enhanced because you will not need to worry so much about breaks on the green.

2 Control the pace of your putt with the length of your backswing. Go to a putting green and work out how far each length of backswing hits a putt. Make a note of them and consciously work on keeping your rhythm and tempo accurate. When you are faced with longer putts, all you have to do is recall the correct backswing.

Byron Nelson was one of the steadiest golf players. Although he won five major championships, it was his reliability in regular US PGA Tour events that caught the eye. For example, he won the 1939 Western Open without missing a fairway over 72 holes. Consistency on the green was also key to his success – he would three-putt only rarely.

Pro tip

When faced with a long putt, think what you need to do. Say to yourself: 'Knock this one dead', or 'Let's sink this one'. Positive thoughts lead to a positive stroke. Tell yourself: 'Let's hit this on the green'. It is hopeless saying to yourself: 'Don't three-putt' because all you will be thinking about is three-putting.

3 Hover the putter at address, to smooth out your stroke over longer distances and caress the ball rather than hit at it. This will avoid mishits and duffed putts. Make practice strokes like this, feeling the freedom of movement. Make the putt without resting the putterhead on the grass; your stroke becomes fluid.

4 If you find yourself struggling with long putts, trust your technique and blank your mind; try not to think too hard. If you over-think the distance, you will lose all natural feel and instinct in your stroke. Golf becomes difficult when it gets conscious. Make your technique as reactive as possible, and let your senses do the work.

Chipping
practice

Seve Ballesteros is the most iconic of all European golfers and his charisma, energy and style are single-handedly responsible for the European Tour being a viable place to earn a living as a professional golfer. Seve is one of few golfers to have an event named after him. The Seve Trophy is a biannual team event between Great Britain & Ireland and Continental Europe. At its second staging, in 2002 at Druids Glen in Ireland, Seve defeated Colin Montgomerie in the singles through his short game. He missed most fairways and greens but got up-and-down from everywhere, to overcome an exasperated Monty 2&1.

Seve
Ballesteros

Country Spain

Born 9 April 1957

Notable achievements
Open Championship winner 1979, 1984, 1988; US Masters winner 1980, 1983; Ryder Cup 1979, 1983, 1985, 1987, 1989, 1991, 1993, 1995, (captain) 1997

Seve Ballesteros' remarkable touch and ability around the greens emerged from the way he learned the game. He had only a 3-iron to play with, so developed all sorts of weird and wonderful ways of getting the ball close to the hole. He would also spend hours on the beach with his club, not only perfecting bunker play but also working on his ball striking. As well as five majors, Seve won the European Order of Merit six times and the World Matchplay five times. He formed a formidable and successful partnership with José Maria Olazábal in the Ryder Cup. Nowadays, Seve runs a golf-course design business as well as organizing events.

How to follow Seve's short-game practice tips

Seve Ballesteros can still amaze crowds with his touch and skill around greens. He gives many demonstrations and clinics each year and, although his full swing is not what it was, his short game is still intact. Here are a few things you can learn from the master of chipping.

1 Practise out of as many different lies as possible around the green and try out as many different types of shot as you can imagine from these situations. The most important factor when assessing what shot to play around the greens is the lie, and this routine will open up the options.

2 Grip down the club more, in order to gain extra feel and so get closer to the pin. Another simple technical thought from Seve is to concentrate on your left elbow when you are chipping. Hold it firm throughout the chipping stroke. To help keep the clubface square, picture the elbow driving towards the hole.

3 Let your body and wrists take over and feel the stroke, and become more artistic and fluid in the stroke; don't be as scientific as the orthodox technique suggests. One of the world's top coaches, Jim McLean, noticed that Seve and other top chippers use their body, legs and wrists more in the stroke than normal coaching advocates.

4 Practise chipping on the beach or off firm sand. This is how Seve learned to play, and it is a great way of improving not only your bunker play but also your ball-striking ability.

Pro tip

If you are starting to play golf, devote a large amount of time to perfecting your chipping and putting before seriously working on your full swing. Seve Ballesteros and José Maria Olazábal learned to chip and putt before they tackled their long game. Such an approach also highlights the importance of the short game.

Bunker
practice

In order to win 166 tournaments worldwide you have to be a decent bunker player. And if you are the greatest bunker player in the world, then you have nothing to fear with most approach shots you play. So it was with Gary Player, but there was a reason he was so good: practice.

Perfecting
bunker play

Gary Player is always keen to pass on advice and tips. When heckled by the crowd who were tired of his miraculous bunker escapes, claiming he was the luckiest golfer they had seen, Gary coined the most famous sporting phrase since the Second World War when he replied: 'You know, it is funny but the more I practise the luckier I get.' This has become his motto for life. Gary also lives by 'Ten Commandments' (as published on his website). Two seem particularly applicable to bunker play: 'Persistence and common sense are more important than intelligence' (that is, you do not need to be brilliantly talented – you can work at it); and 'Trust instinct to the end, though you cannot render any reason' (meaning let your natural feel and touch take over around the green – do not paralyse it with over-analysis and a scientific approach).

How to follow Gary's bunker practice

Gary Player advocates working hard at the game, particularly in the bunkers. Bunker practice drills can hone your technique as well as making an hour spent in the sand more enjoyable. Here are some drills that should improve your bunker play and boost your confidence from these tricky spots.

Circle in the sand

1 Drop a ball in the sand and draw a small circle around it, about 15 cm (6 in) in diameter. Then address the ball as you would for a normal bunker shot, using an open stance, the clubface aimed directly at the target and your feet shuffled into the sand.

2 Try to hit through the circle you have drawn, while making a swing; don't concentrate on the ball itself. In a decent bunker shot from a good lie, there is never any need to make contact with the ball. You simply lift that circle's sand out of the bunker and the ball will float with it. This drill will help build confidence.

Pro tip

Make use of all the clubs in your bag. Sand-wedges are specifically designed to help you escape from a bunker, using the appropriate technique. They have specially rounded soles to help scoop sand and your ball. So work on your sand-wedge technique, and don't use a 9-iron or pitching wedge to get out of a bunker.

The line drill

1 Line up six balls, making sure there is enough space for you to strike them independently. Mark a line behind these balls with a bunker rake, so there is 5 cm (2 in) space between the line and the balls.

2 Hit the nearest ball out of the bunker, by striking the sand line behind the ball. Move down the line, hitting all the balls out and just using instinct, natural rhythm and the line in the sand to make the escape.

Practising
difficult shots

Laura Davies is one of the most recognizable figures in women's European golf. Since she turned professional in 1985, she has amassed more than $3 million in prize money and has broken countless scoring records on both sides of the Atlantic. Yet her flamboyant, high-risk style can sometimes cause her problems on the course.

Laura Davies

Country England

Born 5 October 1963

Notable achievements
US Women's Open Championship winner 1987; LPGA Championship winner 1994, 1996; du Maurier Classic winner 1996; Solheim Cup 1990, 1992, 1994, 1996, 1998, 2000, 2002, 2003, 2005

Laura Davies has a high-octane swing and high-octane life. She enjoys fast cars and football as well as creating daring shots on the golf course. She won her first tournament in her first year on the LET (Ladies European Tour) in 1985, picked up four events the next year and claimed her first major in 1987 – the US Women's Open Championship. In 1994 Laura became the first golfer, man or woman, to win on five different Tours in one calendar year, and she has also played in every Solheim Cup since its inception. She has finished in the top ten on the LET Order of Merit every year except two in the last 15 seasons, and she has never permanently been enticed away to play in the more lucrative US LPGA (Ladies Professional Golf Association) Tour. Many people believe that without Laura's influence the LET would have floundered and disappeared forever.

How to follow Laura's troubleshooting

Laura Davies may not have had many golf lessons in her life, but she has spent hours on the range. It is not only drilling the obvious that is essential, especially when you are prone to the occasional wild drive, Laura will also prepare for all eventualities by practising awkward shots.

Conquer slopes

Find a part of the range that is sloping and hit balls from this. Work out the best techniques for this situation, whether it is uphill or downhill, with the ball above or below your feet. See how the ball reacts in each situation and become used to hitting from it. You will quickly boost your confidence.

Roughing it

Locate a thick piece of rough ground on a quiet hole, then lob a dozen balls in the air so they scatter randomly. Some will sit up in fluffy lies, while others will get buried in grass. Hit all the balls at a nearby green and watch how each ball flies from a particular lie and how it reacts when it hits a putting surface.

Practise a crisis

Do a similar drill in the bushes. Throw six balls into a wooded area that does not have too much undergrowth. Go and find each ball and work out what the best shot might be. It could be a left-handed stroke, you might have to use your putter, or you might have to engineer a snap hook around a tree.

Horror bunker shots

Bury a handful of balls in bunkers, giving yourself some tough, plugged lies. The best way to escape a plugged lie is to take a sharper-edged club – a pitching wedge or 9-iron – close the face and chop down into the bottom of the bunker, digging the ball out of the sand. Hit hard and positively, and don't hold back on this shot or worry about a follow-through.

Pro tip

At the end of a session on a grass range, place a dozen balls in any divots you have made, and hit out of them. You will not always find a perfect lie on the middle of the fairway, so it is best to prepare for the worst situation.

Index

Acknowledgements

Executive Editor Trevor Davies
Project Editor Charlotte Macey
Executive Art Editor Darren Southern
Designer Nigel Soper
Senior Production Controller Martin Croshaw
Picture Researcher Emma O'Neill

Thanks to our models Mark Griffiths, Michael Evans and
Victoria Ferris, and to the team at Burhill Golf Club.

Picture Acknowledgements
Special photography: © Octopus Publishing Group
Limited/Angus Murray.

Other photography: Action Plus 12. Colorsport 68, 72. Empics
16, 58, 80, 104; /AP 119 top. Getty Images 38; /Simon Bruty
94; /David Cannon 44, 50, 63 top, 67 top, 77 top; /Central
Press 22; /Mark Dadswell 70; /Stephen Dunn 18; /David Duval
40; /Don Emmert 20; /Ray Floyd 114; /Stuart Franklin 82;
/Jeff Gross 36, 78 bottom, 92; /Scott Halleran 14; /Jeff
Haynes 96; /Harry How 74; /Hulton Archive/Express
Newspapers 49 top; /Phil Inglis 122; /Rusty Jarrett 102;
/Craig Jones 106; /Ross Kinnaird 60, 84; /Kirby 8; /Andy
Lyons 100; /Ronald Martinez 52; /Chris McGrath 113 top;
/Darren McNamara 124; /Donald Miralle 6, 56; /Stephen
Munday 34, 120; /Gary Newkirk 43 top; /Andrew Redington
10, 32, 87 top; /Paul Severn 30; /Jamie Squire 98; /Ronald
Startup 116; /Anna Zieminski 110. Brian Morgan 108. Phil
Sheldon Golf Picture Library 47 top, 54, 65 top, 88; /Dale
Concannon Collection 24; /Ed Lacey 90.
visionsingolf.com/Mark Newcombe 26, 28.